Copyright Page

Mastering Dependency Injection in .NET 8: Advanced Concepts and Patterns
© 2024 Roshan Gavandi

All rights reserved. No part of this book may be reproduced, stored in a retrieval system, or transmitted in any form or by any means electronic, mechanical, photocopying, recording, or otherwise without prior written permission from the publisher, except for brief quotations included in reviews or articles.

Published by: Self-Published

ISBN: 9798301826368

Disclaimer:
The author and publisher have made every effort to ensure the accuracy of the information contained in this book. However, they assume no responsibility for errors, omissions, or inaccuracies. The information in this book is provided "as is" without any warranty, either expressed or implied. The use of the information or materials contained in this book is solely at the user's discretion and risk.

Trademarks:
All trademarks referenced in this book are the property of their respective owners. References to specific software, tools, or libraries do not constitute endorsement or sponsorship by their respective companies.

Printed in US

Mastering Dependency Injection in .NET 8: Advanced Concepts and Patterns

Preface

Dependency Injection (DI) has transformed modern software development, enabling developers to build modular, testable, and maintainable applications. As systems grow in complexity and scale, the ability to manage dependencies effectively has become more critical than ever. This book, *Mastering Dependency Injection in .NET 8: Advanced Concepts and Patterns*, is designed to provide a comprehensive understanding of DI, from foundational principles to advanced techniques, tailored for today's fast-evolving technology landscape.

Why This Book?

With the introduction of .NET 8, Dependency Injection has reached new heights of versatility and performance. However, understanding its nuances and mastering its capabilities often require more than a surface-level exploration. This book bridges the gap between basic knowledge and expert-level proficiency, offering:

- **Practical Examples**: Step-by-step code implementations for real-world scenarios.
- **Advanced Patterns**: Detailed discussions on design patterns like Factory, Strategy, and Decorator, integrated with DI.
- **Cloud-Native Focus**: Techniques for leveraging DI in microservices, serverless applications, and Kubernetes-based architectures.
- **Performance Insights**: Tips and best practices for optimizing DI in large-scale and high-performance systems.

Who Should Read This Book?

This book is for:

- **Software Developers**: Seeking to write cleaner, more maintainable code using DI principles.

- **Cloud Architects**: Implementing DI in distributed systems, microservices, and serverless applications.
- **Technical Leads and Architects**: Looking to introduce or refine DI-based architectures within their teams.
- **Students and Enthusiasts**: Eager to gain a deep understanding of DI and its applications in modern software engineering.

What Will You Learn?

By the end of this book, you will:

1. Understand the core principles and benefits of Dependency Injection.
2. Master the built-in DI framework in .NET 8 and its integration with advanced patterns.
3. Explore real-world applications of DI in microservices, cloud-native systems, and distributed architectures.
4. Optimize DI for performance and scalability in enterprise-grade systems.
5. Anticipate future trends in DI and prepare for upcoming challenges in the field.

A Journey of Exploration

This book is structured to guide you progressively:

- The foundational chapters introduce DI concepts and their implementation in .NET 8.
- Intermediate sections cover practical scenarios, including testing, monitoring, and integrating DI in cloud-native applications.
- Advanced chapters delve into patterns, performance optimizations, and cutting-edge DI trends.
- Throughout the book, examples are crafted with simplicity and relevance, ensuring clarity without oversimplification.

Mastering Dependency Injection in .NET 8: Advanced Concepts and Patterns

-

About the Author

Roshan Gavandi is a distinguished software architect, thought leader, and author with over decades of experience in designing and implementing scalable, secure, and high-performance software systems. A TOGAF-certified professional, Roshan specializes in cloud-native architectures, microservices, distributed systems, and advanced design patterns.

With a strong academic foundation, Roshan holds a **Master of Computer Applications (MCA)** degree and has honed his leadership and business acumen through executive education at the prestigious **Indian Institute of Management Kozhikode (IIMK)**.

Roshan's expertise spans a wide range of technologies, including .NET, Azure, Kubernetes, and Terraform, making him a trusted advisor to organizations navigating complex digital transformations. His ability to simplify intricate concepts has earned him accolades as both an architect and a mentor.

In addition to authoring this comprehensive book on Dependency Injection, Roshan is the author of the acclaimed *Selective Service-Oriented Architecture (SSOA) and Selective Frontend Architecture (SFA): Revolutionizing Modern Software Systems,* which has been widely appreciated for its practical insights and forward-thinking approach.

When not architecting solutions or writing, Roshan shares his knowledge and industry insights through his popular blog: https://roshancloudarchitect.me/

Driven by a passion for learning and teaching, Roshan believes in empowering developers and architects to design systems that are not only robust but also adaptable to the ever-changing technological landscape.

For more insights and resources, visit his blog or connect through professional networks.

Mastering Dependency Injection in .NET 8: Advanced Concepts and Patterns

Acknowledgments

Writing this book has been a rewarding journey, filled with learning, collaboration, and inspiration. Dependency Injection, a cornerstone of modern software development, has evolved significantly over the years. This book is a culmination of countless discussions, real-world implementations, and the collective wisdom of the global developer community.

Gratitude to the Community

To the .NET community and beyond—your contributions, open-source efforts, and shared knowledge have been invaluable. The collaborative spirit of developers worldwide has made this book possible. From insightful blog posts to detailed GitHub repositories, the community has provided endless resources and inspiration.

Special Thanks

1. **Reviewers and Mentors**:
   - Thank you to the technical reviewers who ensured the content was accurate, relevant, and practical.
   - A heartfelt thanks to mentors and peers who challenged my understanding and encouraged me to explore deeper concepts.
2. **Microsoft and the .NET Team**:
   - The advancements in .NET 8 and its DI framework have been game-changing. This book owes much to the robust tools and technologies developed by the .NET team.
3. **Family and Friends**:
   - To my family and friends, your support, patience, and encouragement have been the foundation of this journey. Thank you for believing in this vision.

4. **Readers**:
    - To you, the reader — thank you for embarking on this journey with me. Your curiosity and commitment to learning are what drive the growth of our field.

Inspiration

This book is dedicated to developers who strive for excellence in their craft. It is inspired by the challenges we face every day: building scalable systems, solving complex problems, and constantly evolving to meet the demands of the industry. Your determination to innovate and create better software systems fuels the passion behind this work.

Collaborators and Tools

- **Open-Source Tools and Libraries**:
    - Special thanks to libraries like Scrutor, Autofac, and others that extend and enrich the Dependency Injection ecosystem.
- **Documentation and Resources**:
    - Official documentation, blogs, and forums have been instrumental in shaping the ideas presented in this book.

As you dive into the chapters of this book, I hope it equips you with the tools and insights to tackle modern software challenges with confidence. This journey of exploration and innovation is a shared one, and I look forward to seeing how you apply these principles in your projects.

Here's to building better, smarter, and more resilient software systems together.

Introduction

Why Dependency Injection?

Software development has evolved dramatically, moving from monolithic architectures to microservices, serverless computing, and cloud-native systems. In this new paradigm, the ability to design scalable, maintainable, and testable applications is more critical than ever. Dependency Injection (DI) plays a pivotal role in achieving these goals by decoupling components, promoting modularity, and streamlining dependency management.

The Purpose of This Book

Dependency Injection is more than a technical concept—it is a design philosophy that empowers developers to create flexible and resilient software systems. This book aims to take you on a journey from understanding the fundamentals of DI to mastering advanced patterns and real-world applications, especially in the context of .NET 8.

In this book, you will learn:

- The foundational principles of DI and its benefits in modern software design.
- How to effectively use the built-in DI framework in .NET 8.
- Advanced techniques like service decoration, keyed services, and contextual dependency resolution.
- Integrating DI with cloud-native tools like Kubernetes, Azure Functions, and AWS Lambda.
- Best practices for testing, monitoring, and optimizing DI in enterprise-grade applications.

Who Is This Book For?

This book is for a wide range of readers:

1. **Beginner Developers**: If you're new to DI, this book will help you understand the basics and progressively build your expertise.
2. **Experienced Engineers**: Dive into advanced patterns, optimizations, and real-world scenarios.
3. **Cloud Architects and Technical Leads**: Learn to leverage DI for building scalable, maintainable, and cloud-native systems.
4. **Students and Enthusiasts**: Gain insights into DI concepts and their relevance in modern software engineering.

What Makes This Book Unique?

1. **Practical Approach**:
   - Theoretical explanations are paired with step-by-step examples to ensure clarity and applicability.
2. **Real-World Scenarios**:
   - Every concept is grounded in real-world use cases, from microservices to serverless systems.
3. **Focus on .NET 8**:
   - The book is tailored to the latest advancements in .NET 8, including its DI enhancements.
4. **Advanced Techniques**:
   - Topics like service factories, contextual DI, and integration with cloud platforms are covered in depth.

How to Navigate This Book

The book is structured to guide you through a logical progression of learning:

1. **Foundations**: The early chapters establish a solid understanding of DI concepts and their implementation in .NET 8.
2. **Intermediate Concepts**: Subsequent chapters delve into practical applications, testing, and monitoring.
3. **Advanced Techniques**: Explore complex design patterns, performance optimizations, and cutting-edge DI trends.
4. **Real-World Applications**: The final chapters focus on cloud-native DI, integrating DI with distributed systems, and future trends.

Each chapter is designed to stand alone, allowing you to refer back to specific topics as needed.

Why Now?

With .NET 8, Dependency Injection has reached a level of maturity that makes it indispensable for modern software systems. The latest features—such as enhanced performance, lightweight containers, and support for emerging architectures—make this the perfect time to master DI.

What You Will Gain

By the end of this book, you will:

1. Build a strong foundation in Dependency Injection.
2. Understand advanced patterns and their practical applications.

3. Integrate DI seamlessly into cloud-native and distributed systems.
4. Optimize DI for performance, scalability, and maintainability.
5. Anticipate and prepare for future trends in DI.

A Shared Journey

This book is not just about learning it's about evolving as a developer. Whether you're a seasoned professional or a curious beginner, the journey ahead will empower you to tackle the challenges of modern software development with confidence.

Let's begin this journey together and unlock the full potential of Dependency Injection

Index

Copyright Page 1

Preface 3

Why This Book? — 3

Who Should Read This Book? — 3

What Will You Learn? — 4

A Journey of Exploration — 4

About the Author 6

Acknowledgments 9

Gratitude to the Community — 9

Special Thanks — 9

Inspiration — 10

Collaborators and Tools — 10

Introduction 11

Why Dependency Injection? — 11

The Purpose of This Book — 11

Who Is This Book For? — 12

What Makes This Book Unique? — 12

How to Navigate This Book — 12

Why Now? — 13

What You Will Gain — 13

A Shared Journey — 14

Chapter 1: Introduction to Dependency Injection in .NET 29

Introduction	29
What is Dependency Injection?	29

Key Principles of DI — 29
- Why Dependency Injection Matters — 30
- Dependency Injection in .NET — 30

Key Features of DI in .NET — 31
- Setting Up Dependency Injection in .NET — 31

Step 1: Define an Interface — 31
Step 2: Implement the Interface — 31
Step 3: Register the Service — 32
Step 4: Resolve and Use the Service — 32
- Advanced DI Concepts — 32
  - Preparing for Keyed Services — 33
  - Summary — 33

Chapter 2: Basics of Keyed Services in .NET 8 35

Introduction	35
What are Keyed Services?	35
Key Concepts	35
Why Keyed Services Matter	36
How to Use Keyed Services in .NET 8	36

Step 1: Define a Service Interface — 36
Step 2: Create Multiple Implementations — 37
Step 3: Register Services with Keys — 37
Step 4: Resolve Services Dynamically — 38
- Output — 38
  - Real-World Use Cases — 39
  - Advanced Scenarios — 39
  - Testing Keyed Services — 41
  - Summary — 42

Chapter 3: Managing Service Lifetimes in Dependency Injection 43

Introduction	43
Overview of Service Lifetimes	43
Registering Service Lifetimes	44
Keyed Services and Service Lifetimes	44

Example: Registering Keyed Services with Different Lifetimes — 44
- Resolving Services with Mixed Lifetimes — 45

Best Practices for Using Service Lifetimes — 45

Advanced Concepts — 46

1. Lifetime Mismatches — 46
2. Handling Multi-Threaded Applications — 47
3. Service Lifetimes in Background Tasks — 48
   - Real-World Use Cases — 49

Common Mistakes and How to Avoid Them — 49

Summary — 49

Chapter 4: Conditional Dependency Injection 51

Introduction — 51

What is Conditional Dependency Injection? — 51

Common Scenarios for CDI — 51

Implementing Conditional Dependency Injection — 52

1. Using IServiceProvider — 52
2. Using Keyed Services — 53
3. Using Factories — 54
4. Using Configuration Settings — 55
   - Advanced Scenarios — 56

1. Combining CDI with Middleware — 56
2. CDI in Background Services — 56
   - Best Practices — 58

Common Pitfalls — 58

Summary — 59

Chapter 5: Design Patterns with Dependency Injection 61

Introduction — 61

1. Strategy Pattern — 61

Overview — 61
Example: Payment Processing — 62
2. Factory Pattern — 63

Overview — 63
Example: Notification Service — 64
3. Chain of Responsibility — 65

Overview — 65
Example: Logging Pipeline — 66
4. State Pattern — 68

Overview — 68
Example: Order State Management — 68
Summary — 70

Chapter 6: Dependency Injection in Middleware 71

Introduction — 71

Understanding Middleware — 71

Integrating DI in Middleware — 72

1. Injecting Services into Middleware — 72
2. Using Scoped Services in Middleware — 72
3. Resolving Scoped Services Dynamically — 73
Advanced Scenarios — 74

1. Multi-Tenant Middleware — 74
2. Middleware with Feature Toggles — 75
3. Combining Middleware with Keyed Services — 77
Testing Middleware with DI — 78

Best Practices — 78

Summary — 79

Chapter 7: Dependency Injection with gRPC 81

Introduction — 81

gRPC Basics and DI — 81

Injecting Dependencies into gRPC Services	82
Using Scoped Services in gRPC	83
Injecting Dependencies into gRPC Clients	84
Advanced Scenarios	85

1. Multi-Environment gRPC Clients — 85
2. Combining Keyed Services with gRPC — 86
   Best Practices — 87

Testing gRPC with DI	88
Summary	89

Chapter 8: Using Dependency Injection in Hosted Background Services 91

Introduction	91
Understanding Hosted Services	91
Basic Integration of DI with Hosted Services	92

1. Creating a Simple Hosted Service — 92
   2. Using Scoped Services in Hosted Services — 92

   3. Handling Multi-Threaded Tasks — 94

   Advanced Scenarios — 95

1. Using Keyed Services in Background Tasks — 95
2. Combining Timers with DI — 96
   Testing Hosted Services — 97

Best Practices	98
Summary	99

Chapter 9: Cross-Cutting Concerns with Dependency Injection 101

Introduction	101
1. Logging with DI	101

Centralized Logging — 101
Combining Logging with Keyed Services — 102
   2. Caching with DI — 103

Centralized Caching — 103
Distributed Caching with DI — 104
   3. Validation with DI — 105

Validation Service — 105
Middleware-Based Validation — 106
   4. Exception Handling — 107

Centralized Exception Logging — 107
   Advanced Scenarios — 108

Combining Cross-Cutting Concerns — 108
Cross-Cutting Concerns with Keyed Services — 109
   Best Practices — 110

   Summary — 110

Chapter 10: Dynamic Dependency Resolution with Advanced Scenarios 113

   Introduction — 113

   1. Dynamic Resolution with IServiceProvider — 113

Example: Resolving Services Dynamically — 113
   2. Using Keyed Services for Dynamic Resolution — 115

   3. Runtime Service Registration — 116

   4. Custom Service Providers — 117

   5. Real-World Use Cases — 117

Multi-Tenant Applications — 118
Feature Toggles — 118
Dynamic Middleware — 119
   Best Practices — 120

   Summary — 121

Chapter 11: Performance Optimization and Debugging in Dependency Injection..........123

   Introduction — 123

   1. Performance Considerations in DI — 123

1.1 Service Resolution Overhead — 123
1.2 Large Object Graphs — 124

1.3 Improper Service Lifetimes   124
    2. Optimizing Service Registration and Resolution   124

2.1 Minimize Use of **Transient** Services   124
2.2 Use Factories for Expensive Objects   124
2.3 Precompute Dependencies   125
2.4 Register Services Explicitly   126
    3. Debugging DI-Related Issues   126

3.1 Common Issues   126
3.2 Service Not Registered   127
3.3 Lifetime Mismatch   127
    4. Tools and Techniques for Analyzing DI Performance   128

4.1 Built-in Logging   128
4.2 Diagnostic Tools   128
4.3 Profiling Tools   128
    5. Real-World Examples   129

5.1 Debugging a Circular Dependency   129
5.2 Resolving a Performance Bottleneck   130
    Best Practices   130

    Summary   131

Chapter 12: Designing Modular and Extensible Applications with Dependency Injection 133

    Introduction   133

    1. Principles of Modular and Extensible Design   133

    2. Leveraging DI for Modularity   134

Example: Modular User Management System   134
    3. Extending Applications Dynamically with DI   136

Example: Adding Plugins at Runtime   136
    4. Real-World Architectural Patterns   137

4.1 Plugin Architecture   137
4.2 Microservices   138
4.3 Feature Modules   139
    5. Advanced DI Techniques for Loose Coupling   140

5.1 Using Factories for Modular Dependencies — 140
5.2 Dynamic Resolution for Feature Toggles — 140
   Best Practices — 141

   Summary — 141

Chapter 13: Integrating Dependency Injection in Cross-Platform Applications 143

   Introduction — 143

   1. DI in Mobile Applications — 143

1.1 Dependency Injection in Xamarin and .NET MAUI — 143
1.2 Platform-Specific Implementations — 145
   2. DI in Desktop Applications — 145

2.1 Using DI in WPF — 146
2.2 Using DI in WinForms — 147
   3. DI in Cloud-Native Applications — 148

3.1 Azure Functions — 148
3.2 AWS Lambda — 149
   4. Best Practices for Cross-Platform Dependency Management — 150

   5. Advanced Techniques for Platform-Specific Resolution — 151

Using Factories for Platform-Specific Services — 151
   Summary — 151

Chapter 14: EF Core for Service Factory in Background Services 153

   Introduction — 153

   1. Leveraging EF Core in Background Services — 153

Challenges — 153
Solution — 154
   2. Implementing a Service Factory for EF Core — 154

   3. Using EF Core in a Background Service — 155

   4. Advanced Scenarios — 156

4.1 Multi-Tenant Database Operations — 156
4.2 Batch Processing — 157
   5. Best Practices — 157

6. Real-World Use Case	158
Summary	159

Chapter 15: Testing and Mocking with Dependency Injection 161

Introduction	161
1. Testing Strategies with DI	161
1.1 Unit Testing	161
1.2 Integration Testing	162
1.3 End-to-End Testing	162
2. Mocking Dependencies for Unit Tests	162
2.1 Using Moq for Mocking	162
2.2 Mocking Multiple Dependencies	163
3. Setting Up DI for Integration Tests	164
3.1 Using In-Memory Databases	165
3.2 Configuring Dependency Injection for Integration Tests	165
4. Real-World Testing Scenarios	166
4.1 Testing Background Services	166
4.2 Testing Middleware	167
5. Best Practices	169
Summary	169

Chapter 16: Design Patterns with Advanced Dependency Injection......171

Introduction	171
1. Mediator Pattern with DI	171
Overview	171
2. Proxy Pattern with DI	173
Overview	173
3. Composite Pattern with DI	174
Overview	175
4. Decorator Pattern with DI	176
Overview	176
5. Real-World Scenarios	178

Best Practices 178

Summary 179

Chapter 17: Advanced Techniques with Dependency Injection - Service Decoration and Dynamic Registration 181

Introduction 181

1. Understanding Service Decoration 181

How It Works 181

Use Cases 182

1.1 Implementing Service Decoration 182

Step 1: Define the Service Interface and Implementation 182
Step 2: Create the Decorator 182
Step 3: Register Services with Decoration 183
1.2 Chaining Multiple Decorators 183

2. Dynamic Service Registration 184

2.1 Dynamic Registration Example 185

2.2 Runtime Replacement of Services 185

2.3 Real-Time Registration in Middleware 186

3. Combining Service Decoration and Dynamic Registration 187

Example: Multi-Tenant Service Decoration 187

Real-World Scenario: Feature Toggles with Decorators 187

4. Best Practices 188

Summary 189

Chapter 18: Design Patterns with Advanced Dependency Injection 191

Introduction 191

1. Factory Pattern with DI 191

Implementation 191

2. Strategy Pattern with DI 193

Implementation 193

3. Decorator Pattern with DI 194
Implementation — 194

4. Proxy Pattern with DI 196
Implementation — 196

5. Combining Patterns 197
Example: Caching Decorated Strategies — 197

6. Real-World Scenarios 198
Best Practices — 198

Summary 199

Chapter 19: Optimizing Dependency Injection for Large-Scale Applications 201
Introduction — 201

1. Performance Optimization Techniques 201
1.1 Minimize Service Resolution Overhead — 201

1.2 Use Lazy Initialization — 202

1.3 Profile and Analyze DI Performance — 203

2. Managing Lifecycles Effectively 203
2.1 Choose the Right Lifecycle — 203

2.2 Scoped Services in Background Tasks — 204

2.3 Avoid Circular Dependencies — 204

3. Advanced Configuration and Dynamic Resolution 205
3.1 Register Services Dynamically — 205

3.2 Use Keyed Services for Context-Specific Implementations — 206

4. Handling Common Pitfalls in DI 206
4.1 Overusing DI — 206

4.2 Memory Leaks — 207

5. Best Practices for Large-Scale DI 207
Summary 208

Chapter 20: Dependency Injection in Cloud-Native Microservices 209

Introduction — 209

1. Dependency Injection in Containerized Microservices 209

1.1 Setting Up DI in a Containerized Microservice — 209

1.2 Multi-Tenant Microservices with DI — 211

2. Integrating DI with Kubernetes 212

2.1 Using Kubernetes ConfigMaps and Secrets with DI — 212

2.2 Health Checks and DI — 213

3. DI in Serverless Architectures 213

3.1 Dependency Injection in Azure Functions — 214

3.2 Dependency Injection in AWS Lambda — 214

4. Real-World Scenarios 215

4.1 Distributed Tracing — 215

4.2 API Gateway Integration — 216

5. Best Practices 216

Summary — 217

Chapter 21: Testing and Monitoring Dependency Injection in Cloud-Native Systems 219

Introduction — 219

1. Unit Testing for DI-Based Services 219

1.1 Mocking Dependencies — 219

1.2 Validating Service Configurations — 220

2. Integration Testing in Distributed Systems 221

2.1 Using In-Memory Databases — 221

2.2 Testing HTTP Interactions — 222

3. Observability with DI 223

3.1 Logging Dependency Usage — 223

3.2 Distributed Tracing — 223

3.3 Monitoring Performance — 224

4. Tools for Monitoring DI 224
5. Best Practices for Testing and Monitoring DI 225
Summary 226
Chapter 21: Future Trends in Dependency Injection 229

Introduction — 229

1. Evolution of DI Frameworks 229

1.1 Key Milestones in DI — 229

1.2 Current State of DI in .NET — 230

2. Emerging Patterns in DI 230

2.1 Contextual Dependency Injection — 230

2.2 Polymorphic Registration — 230

2.3 DI in Event-Driven Architectures — 231

3. Trends in DI for Serverless and Cloud-Native Architectures 232

3.1 Lightweight DI Containers — 232

3.2 Integration with Configuration Services — 232

3.3 DI in Kubernetes — 232

4. DI in Machine Learning and AI 233

4.1 Injecting ML Models — 233

4.2 Managing Model Lifecycles — 233

5. Future Possibilities for DI Frameworks 234

5.1 AI-Assisted DI Configuration — 234

5.2 Predictive Service Resolution — 234

5.3 Fully Decentralized DI — 234

5.4 Enhanced Observability — 234

Best Practices for Preparing for Future DI Trends 234

Summary...235

Appendices..236

Appendix A: Glossary of Terms 236

Appendix B: .NET 8 Dependency Injection Features 236

Appendix C: Tools and Libraries for DI 237

Appendix D: Example Configurations 237

Basic DI Setup 237
Service Decoration 237
Keyed Services 237

Appendix E: Troubleshooting DI 238

Appendix F: Resources for Further Learning 238

Appendix G: Advanced DI Patterns Cheat Sheet 238

Chapter 1: Introduction to Dependency Injection in .NET

Introduction

Dependency Injection (DI) is a fundamental design pattern in software development that promotes loose coupling and improves the maintainability, testability, and scalability of applications. In .NET, DI has become a cornerstone of modern development, evolving over the years to integrate deeply with the framework. With .NET 8, the introduction of Keyed Services brings a new dimension to DI, allowing developers to dynamically resolve services based on specific keys.

This chapter introduces the concept of DI, explains its importance in application design, and explores its evolution within the .NET ecosystem. It also lays the groundwork for understanding advanced features like Keyed Services by delving into the core principles of DI.

What is Dependency Injection?

Dependency Injection is a design pattern that implements the **Inversion of Control (IoC)** principle. Instead of a class creating its dependencies, they are provided (injected) from an external source, typically by a container. This separation of concerns simplifies testing, reduces code duplication, and allows for dynamic behavior changes.

Key Principles of DI

1. **Inversion of Control (IoC):**

- The control of creating and managing dependencies is inverted from the class to an external entity.
2. **Loose Coupling:**
   - Classes depend on abstractions (e.g., interfaces) rather than concrete implementations.
3. **Service Lifetimes:**
   - Dependencies can have controlled lifetimes (e.g., transient, scoped, singleton) based on the application's needs.

Why Dependency Injection Matters

1. **Testability:**
   - Dependencies can be replaced with mocks or stubs during testing, enabling effective unit testing.
2. **Maintainability:**
   - DI promotes modular design by enforcing single responsibility principles.
3. **Flexibility:**
   - Dependencies can be replaced at runtime, making applications adaptable to changing requirements.
4. **Scalability:**
   - DI frameworks allow for dynamic resolution of services, which is critical in enterprise applications.

Dependency Injection in .NET

.NET has first-class support for DI, which is integrated into the framework itself. The built-in DI container in .NET Core and beyond is simple, lightweight, and designed for extensibility. Developers no longer need third-party libraries to manage dependencies effectively.

Key Features of DI in .NET

1. **Built-in Support:**
    - Available out-of-the-box with no need for external libraries.
2. **Service Registration:**
    - Register services with lifetimes like Transient, Scoped, and Singleton.
3. **Service Resolution:**
    - Automatically resolve dependencies at runtime using the built-in container.

Setting Up Dependency Injection in .NET

Here's a simple example to demonstrate how to set up and use DI in a .NET application.

Step 1: Define an Interface

```
public interface IMessageService
{
    void SendMessage(string message);
}
```

Step 2: Implement the Interface

```
public class EmailMessageService : IMessageService
{
    public void SendMessage(string message)
    {
```

```
        Console.WriteLine($"Email sent: {message}");
    }
}
```

Step 3: Register the Service
```
var builder = WebApplication.CreateBuilder(args);
builder.Services.AddSingleton<IMessageService, EmailMessageService>();

var app = builder.Build();
```

Step 4: Resolve and Use the Service
```
app.MapGet("/send", (IMessageService messageService, string message) =>
{
    messageService.SendMessage(message);
    return Results.Ok("Message sent successfully!");
});

app.Run();
```

Advanced DI Concepts

1. **Service Lifetimes:**
    - **Transient:** Created every time they are requested.
    - **Scoped:** Created once per request.
    - **Singleton:** Created once and shared throughout the application's lifetime.
2. **Nested Dependencies:**

- Services can depend on other services, creating a chain of dependencies.
3. **Service Collections:**
    - Use IServiceCollection to manage all services in the application.
4. **Custom Providers:**
    - Extend the DI container with custom logic for specific resolution scenarios.

Preparing for Keyed Services

Keyed Services build on the foundational concepts of DI, allowing multiple implementations of the same interface to be registered and resolved based on unique keys. Understanding the basics of DI is crucial for exploring advanced features like Keyed Services, which are introduced in Chapter 2.

Summary

Dependency Injection is a powerful pattern that simplifies application design by decoupling dependencies from classes. In .NET, DI has become a standard practice, supported by a robust, built-in container. By mastering the core principles and capabilities of DI, developers can create applications that are easier to maintain, test, and scale.

The next chapter delves into Keyed Services, a new feature in .NET 8 that takes DI to the next level, enabling dynamic resolution of dependencies based on specific keys.

Mastering Dependency Injection in .NET 8: Advanced Concepts and Patterns

Chapter 2: Basics of Keyed Services in .NET 8

Introduction

Keyed Services are a powerful enhancement to the built-in Dependency Injection (DI) framework in .NET 8. They allow developers to register multiple implementations of the same service interface and resolve them dynamically based on unique keys. This feature is particularly valuable in scenarios requiring dynamic service selection, such as multi-tenancy, feature toggles, and environment-specific configurations.

In this chapter, we will explore what Keyed Services are, why they are significant, and how to use them effectively in .NET 8. We will cover their registration, resolution, and practical use cases, complemented by examples and best practices.

What are Keyed Services?

Keyed Services extend the DI container's capabilities by associating each service implementation with a unique key. This allows you to dynamically select and resolve the appropriate service at runtime, based on specific requirements.

Key Concepts

1. **Service Registration with Keys:**

- Services are registered in the DI container with a unique key that distinguishes them from other implementations of the same interface.
2. **Service Resolution with Keys:**
    - At runtime, services can be resolved by their associated keys using the container's new GetRequiredKeyedService or TryGetKeyedService methods.
3. **Dynamic Behavior:**
    - The ability to resolve services dynamically based on runtime conditions eliminates the need for complex conditional logic in your code.

Why Keyed Services Matter

1. **Simplifies Complex Scenarios:**
    - Reduces the need for switch statements or manual service resolution in multi-implementation scenarios.
2. **Improves Maintainability:**
    - Encapsulates implementation-specific logic within services, keeping the consuming code clean.
3. **Enhances Flexibility:**
    - Makes it easier to add, remove, or modify service implementations without changing core application logic.

How to Use Keyed Services in .NET 8

Step 1: Define a Service Interface

```
public interface INotificationService
{
    void SendNotification(string message);
```

}

Step 2: Create Multiple Implementations

```csharp
public class EmailNotificationService : INotificationService
{
    public void SendNotification(string message)
    {
        Console.WriteLine($"Email sent: {message}");
    }
}

public class SmsNotificationService : INotificationService
{
    public void SendNotification(string message)
    {
        Console.WriteLine($"SMS sent: {message}");
    }
}
```

Step 3: Register Services with Keys

```csharp
var builder = WebApplication.CreateBuilder(args);

builder.Services.AddKeyedSingleton<INotificationService,
EmailNotificationService>("Email");
builder.Services.AddKeyedSingleton<INotificationService,
SmsNotificationService>("SMS");

var app = builder.Build();
```

Step 4: Resolve Services Dynamically

Use the GetRequiredKeyedService method to resolve the appropriate service by its key.

```
app.MapGet("/notify", (IServiceProvider serviceProvider, string notificationType,
string message) =>
{
    try
    {
        var notificationService =
serviceProvider.GetRequiredKeyedService<INotificationService>(notificationType);
        notificationService.SendNotification(message);
        return Results.Ok($"Notification sent via {notificationType}");
    }
    catch (InvalidOperationException)
    {
        return Results.BadRequest($"No service registered for key:
{notificationType}");
    }
});

app.Run();
```

Output

1. **Request:** /notify?notificationType=Email&message=Hello
    - **Console Output:** Email sent: Hello
    - **Response:** Notification sent via Email
2. **Request:** /notify?notificationType=SMS&message=Hello
    - **Console Output:** SMS sent: Hello

- **Response:** Notification sent via SMS

Real-World Use Cases

1. **Multi-Tenancy:**
    - Each tenant can have its own implementation of a service, such as data providers or logging mechanisms.
2. **Feature Toggles:**
    - Enable or disable features dynamically by resolving specific service implementations.
3. **Environment-Specific Behavior:**
    - Use different services for Development, Staging, and Production environments.
4. **API Versioning:**
    - Handle multiple versions of APIs by associating each implementation with a version key.

Advanced Scenarios

1. **Combining Keyed Services with Configuration**
    - Resolve services based on configuration values.

```csharp
public class NotificationManager
{
    private readonly IServiceProvider _serviceProvider;
    private readonly IConfiguration _configuration;
```

```csharp
    public NotificationManager(IServiceProvider serviceProvider, IConfiguration configuration)
    {
        _serviceProvider = serviceProvider;
        _configuration = configuration;
    }

    public void Notify(string message)
    {
        var defaultNotificationType = _configuration["DefaultNotificationType"];
        var service = _serviceProvider.GetRequiredKeyedService<INotificationService>(defaultNotificationType);
        service.SendNotification(message);
    }
}
```

2. **Fallback Strategies with TryGetKeyedService**
    - Handle cases where the requested key is not registered.

```csharp
app.MapGet("/notifyWithFallback", (IServiceProvider serviceProvider, string notificationType, string message) =>
{
    if (!serviceProvider.TryGetKeyedService<INotificationService>(notificationType, out var notificationService))
    {
        notificationService = serviceProvider.GetRequiredKeyedService<INotificationService>("Email"); // Default fallback
    }

    notificationService.SendNotification(message);    return Results.Ok("Notification sent with fallback strategy.");
```

```
});
```

Testing Keyed Services

Mock and test Keyed Services by simulating multiple implementations.

```
[Fact]
public void TestKeyedServiceResolution()
{
    var services = new ServiceCollection();
    var mockEmailService = new Mock<INotificationService>();
    var mockSmsService = new Mock<INotificationService>();

    services.AddKeyedSingleton<INotificationService>(_ => mockEmailService.Object, "Email");
    services.AddKeyedSingleton<INotificationService>(_ => mockSmsService.Object, "SMS");

    var provider = services.BuildServiceProvider();

    var emailService = provider.GetRequiredKeyedService<INotificationService>("Email");
    emailService.SendNotification("Test Email");

    mockEmailService.Verify(x => x.SendNotification("Test Email"), Times.Once);
}
```

Summary

Keyed Services revolutionize Dependency Injection in .NET 8 by enabling dynamic service resolution based on keys. This feature simplifies complex scenarios, improves maintainability, and supports dynamic behavior in modern applications. By mastering the basics of Keyed Services, developers can unlock new possibilities for building flexible and scalable systems.

The next chapter will delve into **Service Lifetimes in Keyed Services**, exploring how to manage the lifecycle of services registered with unique key

Chapter 3: Managing Service Lifetimes in Dependency Injection

Introduction

Service lifetimes are fundamental to Dependency Injection (DI). They define how and when the DI container creates and disposes of services. In .NET, understanding service lifetimes is critical for building efficient and scalable applications, especially when dealing with Keyed Services. Mismanaging service lifetimes can lead to performance issues, memory leaks, or unintended behaviors.

In this chapter, we will explore the three main service lifetimes in .NET: **Transient**, **Scoped**, and **Singleton**. We'll also discuss best practices for using these lifetimes with Keyed Services and delve into advanced concepts such as lifetime mismatches and handling multi-threaded applications.

Overview of Service Lifetimes

1. **Transient:**
    - A new instance is created every time the service is requested.
    - Ideal for lightweight, stateless services.
    - Example: Utility services such as string formatters or mappers.
2. **Scoped:**
    - A single instance is created per scope (e.g., per HTTP request in web applications).
    - Suitable for services that maintain state during a specific operation or request.

- Example: Database contexts in web applications.
3. **Singleton:**
    - A single instance is created for the entire application lifetime.
    - Ideal for services that are shared and do not maintain mutable state.
    - Example: Configuration readers or caching services.

Registering Service Lifetimes

In .NET, you can register services with the following methods:

- AddTransient<TService, TImplementation>()
- AddScoped<TService, TImplementation>()
- AddSingleton<TService, TImplementation>()

When working with Keyed Services, these methods are extended:

- AddKeyedTransient<TService, TImplementation>(key)
- AddKeyedScoped<TService, TImplementation>(key)
- AddKeyedSingleton<TService, TImplementation>(key)

Keyed Services and Service Lifetimes

Keyed Services allow you to register multiple implementations with different lifetimes. This flexibility enables dynamic and efficient service management.

Example: Registering Keyed Services with Different Lifetimes

```
builder.Services.AddKeyedTransient<IMessageService, EmailMessageService>("Email");
builder.Services.AddKeyedScoped<IMessageService, SmsMessageService>("SMS");
```

```
builder.Services.AddKeyedSingleton<IMessageService,
PushNotificationService>("Push");
```

Resolving Services with Mixed Lifetimes

When resolving Keyed Services with different lifetimes, it's essential to ensure compatibility. Here's an example of resolving services dynamically:

```
public class NotificationManager
{
    private readonly IServiceProvider _serviceProvider;

    public NotificationManager(IServiceProvider serviceProvider)
    {
        _serviceProvider = serviceProvider;
    }

    public void Notify(string notificationType, string message)
    {
        var service =
_serviceProvider.GetRequiredKeyedService<IMessageService>(notificationType);
        service.SendMessage(message);
    }
}
```

Best Practices for Using Service Lifetimes

1. **Match Lifetimes Appropriately:**

- Avoid injecting shorter-lived services (e.g., Transient) into longer-lived ones (e.g., Singleton).
2. **Use Scoped Services for Web Applications:**
    - Scoped services are ideal for maintaining request-specific data, such as user context or database transactions.
3. **Leverage Singleton for Global State:**
    - Use Singleton for shared, thread-safe objects like configuration or caching.
4. **Combine Lifetimes Thoughtfully:**
    - Use Keyed Services to mix lifetimes when necessary, ensuring logical isolation between implementations.

Advanced Concepts

1. Lifetime Mismatches

Injecting a transient or scoped service into a singleton can lead to issues. For instance:

```
public class SingletonService
{
    private readonly IScopedService _scopedService;

    public SingletonService(IScopedService scopedService)
    {
        _scopedService = scopedService; // Potential issue
    }
}
```

Solution: Use IServiceProvider to Resolve Scoped Services Dynamically

```
public class SingletonService
```

```csharp
{
    private readonly IServiceProvider _serviceProvider;

    public SingletonService(IServiceProvider serviceProvider)
    {
        _serviceProvider = serviceProvider;
    }

    public void UseScopedService()
    {
        using var scope = _serviceProvider.CreateScope();
        var scopedService =
scope.ServiceProvider.GetRequiredService<IScopedService>();
        scopedService.PerformTask();
    }
}
```

2. Handling Multi-Threaded Applications

Singletons must be thread-safe because they are shared across threads. Use synchronization primitives (e.g., locks) or thread-safe collections.

Example: Thread-Safe Singleton

```csharp
public class ThreadSafeSingleton
{
    private static readonly object _lock = new object();
    private List<string> _data = new List<string>();

    public void AddData(string item)
    {
        lock (_lock)
        {
            _data.Add(item);
```

            }
        }
}

3. Service Lifetimes in Background Tasks

Scoped services are not directly available in background tasks. You must create a new scope explicitly.

Example: Using Scoped Services in a Background Task

```
public class BackgroundWorker : BackgroundService
{
    private readonly IServiceProvider _serviceProvider;

    public BackgroundWorker(IServiceProvider serviceProvider)
    {
        _serviceProvider = serviceProvider;
    }

    protected override async Task ExecuteAsync(CancellationToken stoppingToken)
    {
        while (!stoppingToken.IsCancellationRequested)
        {
            using var scope = _serviceProvider.CreateScope();
            var scopedService = scope.ServiceProvider.GetRequiredService<IScopedService>();
            scopedService.PerformTask();

            await Task.Delay(1000, stoppingToken);
        }
    }
}
```

Real-World Use Cases

1. **Web Applications:**
   - Use Scoped services for request-based operations like user authentication.
2. **Microservices:**
   - Combine Singleton for shared configurations with Scoped for request-based services.
3. **Background Processing:**
   - Resolve scoped dependencies dynamically in hosted services.

Common Mistakes and How to Avoid Them

1. **Avoid Circular Dependencies:**
   - Circular dependencies can cause runtime errors. Refactor services to eliminate direct circular references.
2. **Avoid Overusing Singletons:**
   - Excessive use of singletons can lead to hidden state-sharing issues and reduced testability.
3. **Be Cautious with Scoped Services in Middleware:**
   - Ensure scoped services are resolved within the request pipeline.

Summary

Managing service lifetimes is a crucial aspect of Dependency Injection. By understanding the differences between Transient, Scoped, and Singleton lifetimes, and applying best practices, developers can design efficient and maintainable applications. When combined with Keyed Services, service lifetimes offer unparalleled flexibility in creating dynamic, scalable solutions.

In the next chapter, we will explore **Conditional Dependency Injection**, delving into scenarios where dependencies are resolved based on runtime conditions or configurations.

Chapter 4: Conditional Dependency Injection

Introduction

In real-world applications, the behavior of services often depends on runtime conditions or configurations, such as environment variables, user roles, or tenant-specific settings. Conditional Dependency Injection (CDI) is a powerful approach to dynamically resolve dependencies based on such criteria.

In this chapter, we will explore the principles of Conditional Dependency Injection, demonstrate how it works in .NET 8, and provide practical use cases. We'll also discuss how Keyed Services enhance CDI and how to combine them with other DI features for advanced scenarios.

What is Conditional Dependency Injection?

Conditional Dependency Injection enables the DI container to resolve different service implementations based on runtime conditions. This approach reduces complex conditional logic (e.g., if-else or switch statements) in the application code and centralizes the dependency resolution process.

Common Scenarios for CDI

1. **Environment-Specific Implementations:**
    - Use different services in Development, Staging, or Production.
2. **Feature Toggles:**
    - Enable or disable specific service implementations based on feature flags.
3. **User Role-Specific Behavior:**
    - Resolve different services for admin users vs. regular users.
4. **Multi-Tenancy:**
    - Provide tenant-specific implementations of a service.

Implementing Conditional Dependency Injection

1. Using IServiceProvider

The most straightforward way to implement CDI is by resolving services dynamically using IServiceProvider.

Example: Dynamic Resolution Based on Environment

```
public class PaymentManager
{
    private readonly IServiceProvider _serviceProvider;

    public PaymentManager(IServiceProvider serviceProvider)
    {
        _serviceProvider = serviceProvider;
    }

    public IPaymentService GetPaymentService(string environment)
    {
        if (environment == "Development")
            return _serviceProvider.GetRequiredService<DevPaymentService>();
        else if (environment == "Production")
            return _serviceProvider.GetRequiredService<ProdPaymentService>();
```

```
        throw new InvalidOperationException("Unsupported environment");
    }
}
```

2. Using Keyed Services

Keyed Services simplify CDI by associating each service implementation with a unique key, eliminating the need for manual if-else logic.

Example: Environment-Based Keyed Services

```
public class ProdPaymentService : IPaymentService
{
    public void ProcessPayment(decimal amount) => Console.WriteLine($"Production Payment: {amount:C}");
}

// Service Registration
builder.Services.AddKeyedSingleton<IPaymentService, DevPaymentService>("Development");
builder.Services.AddKeyedSingleton<IPaymentService, ProdPaymentService>("Production");

// Dynamic Resolution
public class PaymentManager
{
    private readonly IServiceProvider _serviceProvider;

    public PaymentManager(IServiceProvider serviceProvider)
    {
        _serviceProvider = serviceProvider;
    }
```

```csharp
    public void HandlePayment(string environment, decimal amount)
    {
        var paymentService =
_serviceProvider.GetRequiredKeyedService<IPaymentService>(environment);
        paymentService.ProcessPayment(amount);
    }
}
```

3. Using Factories

Factories provide a clean abstraction for CDI, especially when conditions are complex or dynamic.

Example: Role-Based Service Factory

```csharp
public class UserRoleServiceFactory
{
    private readonly IServiceProvider _serviceProvider;

    public UserRoleServiceFactory(IServiceProvider serviceProvider)
    {
        _serviceProvider = serviceProvider;
    }

    public IUserService GetService(string role)
    {
        return role switch
        {
            "Admin" => _serviceProvider.GetRequiredService<AdminUserService>(),
            "User" => _serviceProvider.GetRequiredService<RegularUserService>(),
            _ => throw new InvalidOperationException("Invalid role")
        };
    }
}
```

4. Using Configuration Settings

You can integrate CDI with application configuration to resolve services dynamically based on settings.

Example: Configuration-Based Resolution

```
// AppSettings.json
{
  "DefaultPaymentService": "Production"
}

// Service Resolution
public class ConfigBasedServiceResolver
{
    private readonly IServiceProvider _serviceProvider;
    private readonly IConfiguration _configuration;

    public ConfigBasedServiceResolver(IServiceProvider serviceProvider, IConfiguration configuration)
    {
        _serviceProvider = serviceProvider;
        _configuration = configuration;
    }

    public void ProcessPayment(decimal amount)
    {
        var defaultService = _configuration["DefaultPaymentService"];
        var paymentService = _serviceProvider.GetRequiredKeyedService<IPaymentService>(defaultService);
        paymentService.ProcessPayment(amount);
    }
}
```

Advanced Scenarios

1. Combining CDI with Middleware

Use CDI in middleware to resolve services based on headers or query parameters.

Example: Header-Based Service Resolution

```
public class DynamicServiceMiddleware
{
    private readonly RequestDelegate _next;
    private readonly IServiceProvider _serviceProvider;

    public DynamicServiceMiddleware(RequestDelegate next, IServiceProvider serviceProvider)
    {
        _next = next;
        _serviceProvider = serviceProvider;
    }

    public async Task InvokeAsync(HttpContext context)
    {
        var role = context.Request.Headers["Role"];
        var userService = 
_serviceProvider.GetRequiredKeyedService<IUserService>(role);
        context.Items["ResolvedService"] = userService;

        await _next(context);
    }
}
```

2. CDI in Background Services

Use CDI in background tasks to resolve services dynamically based on event types or conditions.

Example: Event-Based Service Resolution

```
public class EventProcessor : BackgroundService
{
    private readonly IServiceProvider _serviceProvider;

    public EventProcessor(IServiceProvider serviceProvider)
    {
        _serviceProvider = serviceProvider;
    }

    protected override async Task ExecuteAsync(CancellationToken stoppingToken)
    {
        while (!stoppingToken.IsCancellationRequested)
        {
            var eventType = GetNextEventType();
            var eventHandler =
_serviceProvider.GetRequiredKeyedService<IEventHandler>(eventType);
            eventHandler.HandleEvent(eventType);

            await Task.Delay(1000, stoppingToken);
        }
    }

    private string GetNextEventType()
    {
        // Simulate dynamic event retrieval
        return DateTime.Now.Second % 2 == 0 ? "OrderCreated" : "OrderCancelled";
    }
}
```

Best Practices

1. **Centralize Conditional Logic:**
   - Use factories or configuration-based resolvers to centralize and simplify conditional dependency logic.
2. **Leverage Keyed Services:**
   - Avoid hardcoding if-else or switch statements by utilizing Keyed Services.
3. **Test Extensively:**
   - Validate all possible runtime conditions to ensure the correct services are resolved.
4. **Use Dependency Inversion:**
   - Depend on abstractions (interfaces) to allow flexibility and extensibility.

Common Pitfalls

1. **Overcomplicating Conditions:**
   - Avoid overly complex conditional logic that is hard to maintain.
2. **Performance Overhead:**
   - Minimize performance impacts by caching frequently resolved services when possible.
3. **Service Resolution Failures:**
   - Handle cases where the requested service key or condition is not supported.

Summary

Conditional Dependency Injection empowers developers to create dynamic, adaptable applications by resolving services based on runtime conditions or configurations. With .NET 8, features like Keyed Services make CDI even more powerful, reducing boilerplate code and improving maintainability. By following best practices and leveraging advanced scenarios, developers can build robust, flexible systems.

In the next chapter, we will explore **Design Patterns with Dependency Injection**, focusing on how DI can simplify the implementation of popular patterns like Strategy, Factory, and Chain of Responsibility.

Mastering Dependency Injection in .NET 8: Advanced Concepts and Patterns

Chapter 5: Design Patterns with Dependency Injection

Introduction

Design patterns are proven solutions to recurring problems in software design. When combined with Dependency Injection (DI), they become more modular, testable, and maintainable. DI simplifies the implementation of many design patterns by automatically resolving dependencies, managing lifetimes, and dynamically selecting services.

This chapter delves into some of the most commonly used design patterns that integrate seamlessly with DI, including:

- **Strategy Pattern**
- **Factory Pattern**
- **Chain of Responsibility**
- **State Pattern**
- **Decorator Pattern**

For each pattern, we will provide in-depth explanations, practical examples, and implementations using DI in .NET 8, including the advanced use of **Keyed Services**.

1. Strategy Pattern

Overview

The Strategy Pattern allows dynamic selection of algorithms or operations at runtime. By injecting different implementations of an interface, DI makes it easy to swap out strategies without altering the consuming code.

Example: Payment Processing

Step 1: Define the Interface

```csharp
public interface IPaymentStrategy
{
    void ProcessPayment(decimal amount);
}
```

Step 2: Implement Different Strategies

```csharp
public class CreditCardPayment : IPaymentStrategy
{
    public void ProcessPayment(decimal amount) =>
        Console.WriteLine($"Processing credit card payment: {amount:C}");
}

public class PayPalPayment : IPaymentStrategy
{
    public void ProcessPayment(decimal amount) =>
        Console.WriteLine($"Processing PayPal payment: {amount:C}");
}
```

Step 3: Register Strategies as Keyed Services

```csharp
builder.Services.AddKeyedSingleton<IPaymentStrategy, CreditCardPayment>("CreditCard");
```

```
builder.Services.AddKeyedSingleton<IPaymentStrategy, PayPalPayment>("PayPal");
```

Step 4: Resolve and Use Strategies

```
public class PaymentProcessor
{
    private readonly IServiceProvider _serviceProvider;

    public PaymentProcessor(IServiceProvider serviceProvider)
    {
        _serviceProvider = serviceProvider;
    }

    public void ProcessPayment(string paymentType, decimal amount)
    {
        var strategy =
_serviceProvider.GetRequiredKeyedService<IPaymentStrategy>(paymentType);
        strategy.ProcessPayment(amount);
    }
}
```

Output

- **Input:** paymentType="CreditCard", amount=100.00
- **Console:** Processing credit card payment: $100.00

2. Factory Pattern

Overview

The Factory Pattern provides an abstraction for object creation, delegating the responsibility to a factory class. DI simplifies this by injecting services dynamically into the factory.

Example: Notification Service

Step 1: Define the Interface

```
public interface INotificationService
{
    void SendNotification(string message);
}
```

Step 2: Implement Services

```
public class EmailNotificationService : INotificationService
{
    public void SendNotification(string message) =>
        Console.WriteLine($"Email sent: {message}");
}

public class SmsNotificationService : INotificationService
{
    public void SendNotification(string message) =>
        Console.WriteLine($"SMS sent: {message}");
}
```

Step 3: Register Services as Keyed Services

```
builder.Services.AddKeyedSingleton<INotificationService,
EmailNotificationService>("Email");
```

```
builder.Services.AddKeyedSingleton<INotificationService,
SmsNotificationService>("SMS");
```

Step 4: Implement the Factory

```
public class NotificationFactory
{
    private readonly IServiceProvider _serviceProvider;

    public NotificationFactory(IServiceProvider serviceProvider)
    {
        _serviceProvider = serviceProvider;
    }

    public INotificationService Create(string type)
    {
        return _serviceProvider.GetRequiredKeyedService<INotificationService>(type);
    }
}
```

Step 5: Use the Factory

```
var factory = app.Services.GetRequiredService<NotificationFactory>();
var service = factory.Create("Email");
service.SendNotification("Hello via Email!");
```

3. Chain of Responsibility

Overview

The Chain of Responsibility pattern allows a request to pass through a chain of handlers. Each handler can process the request or pass it to the next handler.

Example: Logging Pipeline

Step 1: Define the Handler Interface

```
public interface ILogHandler
{
    bool Handle(string logLevel, string message);
}
```

Step 2: Implement Handlers

```
public class InfoLogHandler : ILogHandler
{
    public bool Handle(string logLevel, string message)
    {
        if (logLevel == "Info")
        {
            Console.WriteLine($"INFO: {message}");
            return true;
        }
        return false;
    }
}

public class ErrorLogHandler : ILogHandler
{
    public bool Handle(string logLevel, string message)
    {
        if (logLevel == "Error")
        {
            Console.WriteLine($"ERROR: {message}");
            return true;
```

```
            }
            return false;
        }
    }
}
```

Step 3: Register Handlers with Keys

```
builder.Services.AddKeyedSingleton<ILogHandler, InfoLogHandler>("Info");
builder.Services.AddKeyedSingleton<ILogHandler, ErrorLogHandler>("Error");
```

Step 4: Implement the Chain Processor

```
public class LogProcessor
{
    private readonly IServiceProvider _serviceProvider;
    private readonly List<string> _logKeys = new() { "Info", "Error" };

    public LogProcessor(IServiceProvider serviceProvider)
    {
        _serviceProvider = serviceProvider;
    }

    public void ProcessLog(string logLevel, string message)
    {
        foreach (var key in _logKeys)
        {
            var handler =
_serviceProvider.GetRequiredKeyedService<ILogHandler>(key);
            if (handler.Handle(logLevel, message)) break;
        }
    }
}
```

Output

- **Input:** logLevel="Info", message="System started."
- **Console:** INFO: System started.

---

4. State Pattern

Overview

The State Pattern allows an object to alter its behavior when its internal state changes. DI simplifies the state transitions by injecting the appropriate state implementation dynamically.

Example: Order State Management

Step 1: Define the State Interface

```
public interface IOrderState
{
    void ProcessOrder();
}
```

Step 2: Implement States

```
public class PendingState : IOrderState
{
    public void ProcessOrder() => Console.WriteLine("Order is pending.");
}

public class ApprovedState : IOrderState
{
```

```csharp
    public void ProcessOrder() => Console.WriteLine("Order is approved.");
}
```

Step 3: Register States with Keys

```csharp
builder.Services.AddKeyedSingleton<IOrderState, PendingState>("Pending");
builder.Services.AddKeyedSingleton<IOrderState, ApprovedState>("Approved");
```

Step 4: Resolve States Dynamically

```csharp
public class OrderProcessor
{
    private readonly IServiceProvider _serviceProvider;

    public OrderProcessor(IServiceProvider serviceProvider)
    {
        _serviceProvider = serviceProvider;
    }

    public void Process(string state)
    {
        var orderState = _serviceProvider.GetRequiredKeyedService<IOrderState>(state);
        orderState.ProcessOrder();
    }
}
```

Summary

Design patterns are a natural fit for Dependency Injection, and the integration is further simplified by advanced DI features like Keyed Services in .NET 8. By applying patterns like Strategy, Factory, Chain of Responsibility, and State, developers can create robust and maintainable systems.

In the next chapter, we will explore **Dependency Injection in Middleware**, focusing on how to inject and use services effectively within middleware pipelines.

Chapter 6: Dependency Injection in Middleware

Introduction

Middleware is a central concept in .NET web applications, responsible for handling HTTP requests and responses in a pipeline. Middleware components often require access to services for processing tasks such as authentication, logging, or request modification. Dependency Injection (DI) simplifies middleware development by injecting required services dynamically.

In this chapter, we'll explore how to integrate DI into custom middleware, resolve scoped services dynamically, and address advanced scenarios such as multi-tenant middleware and combining middleware with Keyed Services.

Understanding Middleware

Middleware components are executed in sequence, forming a request-response pipeline. Each middleware can:

1. Process the incoming request.
2. Modify the outgoing response.
3. Short-circuit the pipeline, preventing further execution.

A middleware is typically a class with an Invoke or InvokeAsync method.

Integrating DI in Middleware

1. Injecting Services into Middleware

Example: Logging Middleware

```
public class LoggingMiddleware
{
    private readonly RequestDelegate _next;
    private readonly ILogger<LoggingMiddleware> _logger;

    public LoggingMiddleware(RequestDelegate next, ILogger<LoggingMiddleware> logger)
    {
        _next = next;
        _logger = logger;
    }

    public async Task InvokeAsync(HttpContext context)
    {
        _logger.LogInformation($"Handling request: {context.Request.Path}");
        await _next(context);
        _logger.LogInformation($"Finished handling request: {context.Request.Path}");
    }
}
```

Registration

```
app.UseMiddleware<LoggingMiddleware>();
```

2. Using Scoped Services in Middleware

Scoped services are created per HTTP request. Resolving scoped services in middleware requires careful handling to avoid lifetime mismatches.

Example: Scoped Service Middleware

```
public class RequestLoggerMiddleware
{
    private readonly RequestDelegate _next;

    public RequestLoggerMiddleware(RequestDelegate next)
    {
        _next = next;
    }

    public async Task InvokeAsync(HttpContext context, IRequestLogger requestLogger)
    {
        requestLogger.LogRequest(context.Request.Path);
        await _next(context);
    }
}
```

Registration

```
builder.Services.AddScoped<IRequestLogger, RequestLogger>();
app.UseMiddleware<RequestLoggerMiddleware>();
```

3. Resolving Scoped Services Dynamically

When middleware needs to resolve scoped services at runtime, use IServiceProvider to create a scope.

Example: Dynamic Scoped Service Resolution

```
public class DynamicScopeMiddleware
{
    private readonly RequestDelegate _next;

    public DynamicScopeMiddleware(RequestDelegate next)
    {
        _next = next;
    }

    public async Task InvokeAsync(HttpContext context, IServiceProvider serviceProvider)
    {
        using var scope = serviceProvider.CreateScope();
        var requestLogger = scope.ServiceProvider.GetRequiredService<IRequestLogger>();
        requestLogger.LogRequest(context.Request.Path);

        await _next(context);
    }
}
```

Advanced Scenarios

1. Multi-Tenant Middleware

In multi-tenant applications, middleware can resolve tenant-specific services dynamically using Keyed Services.

Example: Tenant-Specific Middleware

```
public class MultiTenantMiddleware
{
    private readonly RequestDelegate _next;
```

```csharp
    public MultiTenantMiddleware(RequestDelegate next)
    {
        _next = next;
    }

    public async Task InvokeAsync(HttpContext context, IServiceProvider serviceProvider)
    {
        var tenantId = context.Request.Headers["TenantId"].FirstOrDefault();
        if (string.IsNullOrEmpty(tenantId))
        {
            context.Response.StatusCode = 400; // Bad Request
            await context.Response.WriteAsync("TenantId is required.");
            return;
        }

        var tenantService = serviceProvider.GetRequiredKeyedService<ITenantService>(tenantId);
        context.Items["TenantService"] = tenantService;

        await _next(context);
    }
}
```

Registration

```
builder.Services.AddKeyedSingleton<ITenantService, TenantAService>("TenantA");
builder.Services.AddKeyedSingleton<ITenantService, TenantBService>("TenantB");
app.UseMiddleware<MultiTenantMiddleware>();
```

2. Middleware with Feature Toggles

Middleware can resolve services dynamically based on feature toggles or configuration.

Example: Feature-Based Middleware

```csharp
public class FeatureToggleMiddleware
{
    private readonly RequestDelegate _next;
    private readonly IConfiguration _configuration;

    public FeatureToggleMiddleware(RequestDelegate next, IConfiguration configuration)
    {
        _next = next;
        _configuration = configuration;
    }

    public async Task InvokeAsync(HttpContext context, IServiceProvider serviceProvider)
    {
        var featureEnabled = _configuration.GetValue<bool>("FeatureX:Enabled");
        if (featureEnabled)
        {
            var featureService = serviceProvider.GetRequiredService<IFeatureService>();
            featureService.ExecuteFeature();
        }

        await _next(context);
    }
}
```

Registration

```csharp
builder.Services.AddSingleton<IFeatureService, FeatureService>();
app.UseMiddleware<FeatureToggleMiddleware>();
```

3. Combining Middleware with Keyed Services

Middleware can leverage Keyed Services to resolve context-specific dependencies dynamically.

Example: Keyed Logging Middleware

```csharp
public class KeyedLoggingMiddleware
{
    private readonly RequestDelegate _next;

    public KeyedLoggingMiddleware(RequestDelegate next)
    {
        _next = next;
    }

    public async Task InvokeAsync(HttpContext context, IServiceProvider serviceProvider)
    {
        var logType = context.Request.Headers["LogType"];
        var logService = serviceProvider.GetRequiredKeyedService<ILogService>(logType ?? "Default");
        logService.Log($"Request: {context.Request.Path}");

        await _next(context);
    }
}
```

Registration

```csharp
builder.Services.AddKeyedSingleton<ILogService, InfoLogService>("Info");
builder.Services.AddKeyedSingleton<ILogService, ErrorLogService>("Error");
app.UseMiddleware<KeyedLoggingMiddleware>();
```

Testing Middleware with DI

Middleware can be tested in isolation by mocking services and simulating HTTP requests.

Example: Middleware Unit Test

```
[Fact]
public async Task LoggingMiddleware_ShouldLogRequest()
{
    var loggerMock = new Mock<ILogger<LoggingMiddleware>>();
    var middleware = new LoggingMiddleware(context => Task.CompletedTask, loggerMock.Object);

    var context = new DefaultHttpContext();
    context.Request.Path = "/test";

    await middleware.InvokeAsync(context);

    loggerMock.Verify(logger => logger.LogInformation($"Handling request: /test"), Times.Once);
}
```

Best Practices

1. **Avoid Over-Complicating Middleware:**

- Keep middleware focused on a single responsibility.
2. **Use DI for Reusability:**
    - Inject services to enhance modularity and testability.
3. **Handle Scoped Services Carefully:**
    - Always resolve scoped services within the correct scope.
4. **Centralize Middleware Logic:**
    - Use Keyed Services or factories for complex conditions.

Summary

Dependency Injection simplifies middleware by enabling dynamic service resolution and enhancing modularity. Whether you're injecting scoped services, implementing multi-tenant logic, or using Keyed Services for dynamic behavior, DI makes middleware flexible and maintainable. By following best practices, you can build robust middleware pipelines for your applications.

In the next chapter, we'll explore **Dependency Injection with gRPC**, focusing on injecting services into gRPC clients and servers, and handling advanced scenarios like multi-environment configurations.

Mastering Dependency Injection in .NET 8: Advanced Concepts and Patterns

Chapter 7: Dependency Injection with gRPC

Introduction

gRPC (Google Remote Procedure Call) is a high-performance, open-source RPC framework widely adopted for microservices and real-time applications. In .NET, gRPC seamlessly integrates with Dependency Injection (DI), allowing you to inject services into gRPC clients and servers for enhanced modularity, scalability, and maintainability.

This chapter explores how DI works in gRPC applications, covering:

1. Injecting services into gRPC services and clients.
2. Managing service lifetimes in gRPC contexts.
3. Advanced use cases, such as multi-environment configurations and Keyed Services.

gRPC Basics and DI

In a gRPC application:

- **gRPC Servers** expose services that process client requests.
- **gRPC Clients** interact with gRPC servers to invoke remote methods.

.NET's DI container simplifies managing dependencies in both servers and clients, ensuring clean and modular code.

Injecting Dependencies into gRPC Services

gRPC services can directly receive dependencies through constructor injection, just like MVC controllers or middleware.

Example: Injecting a Logger into a gRPC Service

Step 1: Define the gRPC Service

proto

```
syntax = "proto3";

service Greeter {
  rpc SayHello (HelloRequest) returns (HelloReply);
}

message HelloRequest {
  string name = 1;
}

message HelloReply {
  string message = 1;
}
```

Step 2: Implement the Service

```
public class GreeterService : Greeter.GreeterBase
{
    private readonly ILogger<GreeterService> _logger;

    public GreeterService(ILogger<GreeterService> logger)
    {
```

```
        _logger = logger;
    }

    public override Task<HelloReply> SayHello(HelloRequest request,
ServerCallContext context)
    {
        _logger.LogInformation($"Received request from {request.Name}");
        return Task.FromResult(new HelloReply
        {
            Message = $"Hello, {request.Name}"
        });
    }
}
```

Step 3: Register the Service

```
builder.Services.AddSingleton<GreeterService>();
app.MapGrpcService<GreeterService>();
```

Using Scoped Services in gRPC

Scoped services can be injected into gRPC services as long as the lifetime is tied to the request.

Example: Injecting a Scoped Service

```
public class OrderService : Order.OrderBase
{
    private readonly IOrderRepository _orderRepository;
```

```csharp
    public OrderService(IOrderRepository orderRepository)
    {
        _orderRepository = orderRepository;
    }

    public override Task<OrderResponse> GetOrder(OrderRequest request,
ServerCallContext context)
    {
        var order = _orderRepository.GetOrderById(request.Id);
        return Task.FromResult(new OrderResponse
        {
            Id = order.Id,
            Description = order.Description
        });
    }
}
```

Registration

```csharp
builder.Services.AddScoped<IOrderRepository, OrderRepository>();
app.MapGrpcService<OrderService>();
```

Injecting Dependencies into gRPC Clients

gRPC clients can also utilize DI for modular configuration and dynamic service resolution.

Example: Injecting Configuration into a gRPC Client

```csharp
builder.Services.AddGrpcClient<Greeter.GreeterClient>(options =>
{
    options.Address = new Uri("https://localhost:5001");
});
```

Usage in an Application

```
public class GreetingClient
{
    private readonly Greeter.GreeterClient _client;

    public GreetingClient(Greeter.GreeterClient client)
    {
        _client = client;
    }

    public async Task<string> GetGreeting(string name)
    {
        var reply = await _client.SayHelloAsync(new HelloRequest { Name = name });
        return reply.Message;
    }
}
```

Advanced Scenarios

1. Multi-Environment gRPC Clients

Resolve gRPC clients dynamically based on the environment.

Example: Multi-Environment Client

```
builder.Services.AddGrpcClient<Greeter.GreeterClient>("Development", options =>
{
    options.Address = new Uri("https://localhost:5001");
});

builder.Services.AddGrpcClient<Greeter.GreeterClient>("Production", options =>
{
```

```csharp
    options.Address = new Uri("https://api.example.com");
});

public class MultiEnvClient
{
    private readonly IServiceProvider _serviceProvider;

    public MultiEnvClient(IServiceProvider serviceProvider)
    {
        _serviceProvider = serviceProvider;
    }

    public Greeter.GreeterClient GetClient(string environment)
    {
        return _serviceProvider.GetRequiredKeyedService<Greeter.GreeterClient>(environment);
    }
}
```

2. Combining Keyed Services with gRPC

gRPC servers can leverage Keyed Services to handle multi-tenant or feature-specific logic dynamically.

Example: Multi-Tenant gRPC Service

```csharp
public class TenantService : Tenant.TenantBase
{
    private readonly IServiceProvider _serviceProvider;

    public TenantService(IServiceProvider serviceProvider)
    {
        _serviceProvider = serviceProvider;
    }
```

```csharp
    public override Task<TenantResponse> GetTenantData(TenantRequest request, 
ServerCallContext context)
    {
        var tenantService = 
_serviceProvider.GetRequiredKeyedService<ITenantDataService>(request.TenantId);
        var data = tenantService.GetTenantData();

        return Task.FromResult(new TenantResponse { Data = data });
    }
}
```

Registration

```csharp
builder.Services.AddKeyedSingleton<ITenantDataService, TenantAService>("TenantA");
builder.Services.AddKeyedSingleton<ITenantDataService, TenantBService>("TenantB");
app.MapGrpcService<TenantService>();
```

Best Practices

1. **Service Lifetime Management:**
   - Use Scoped services for request-specific dependencies.
   - Avoid injecting Transient services directly into Singleton services.
2. **Centralized Configuration:**
   - Use AddGrpcClient with configuration for centralized management of gRPC client settings.
3. **Leverage Keyed Services:**
   - Use Keyed Services for dynamic multi-tenant or environment-based service resolution.
4. **Test Extensively:**
   - Mock gRPC clients and services during testing to isolate and validate behavior.

Testing gRPC with DI

Mock gRPC services and clients to simulate requests and validate functionality.

Example: Unit Testing a gRPC Service

```
[Fact]
public async Task GreeterService_SayHello_ReturnsExpectedMessage()
{
    var loggerMock = new Mock<ILogger<GreeterService>>();
    var service = new GreeterService(loggerMock.Object);

    var context = new Mock<ServerCallContext>();
    var response = await service.SayHello(new HelloRequest { Name = "John" }, context.Object);

    Assert.Equal("Hello, John", response.Message);
}
```

Example: Unit Testing a gRPC Client

```
[Fact]
public async Task GreetingClient_GetGreeting_ReturnsGreetingMessage()
{
    var mockGreeterClient = new Mock<Greeter.GreeterClient>();
    mockGreeterClient
        .Setup(client => client.SayHelloAsync(It.IsAny<HelloRequest>(), null, null, CancellationToken.None))
        .ReturnsAsync(new HelloReply { Message = "Hello, John" });

    var greetingClient = new GreetingClient(mockGreeterClient.Object);
    var message = await greetingClient.GetGreeting("John");

    Assert.Equal("Hello, John", message);
```

}

Summary

Dependency Injection is an essential tool in gRPC applications, enabling clean separation of concerns, modularity, and dynamic service resolution. By integrating DI with gRPC servers and clients, developers can build scalable, maintainable, and testable systems. Advanced scenarios, such as multi-environment configurations and multi-tenant services, can be easily implemented using DI features like Keyed Services.

In the next chapter, we'll explore **Using Dependency Injection in Hosted Background Services**, focusing on managing long-running tasks and resolving scoped services dynamically.

Mastering Dependency Injection in .NET 8: Advanced Concepts and Patterns

Chapter 8: Using Dependency Injection in Hosted Background Services

Introduction

Background services are critical components of many applications, handling tasks such as periodic data processing, event handling, and cleanup operations. In .NET, IHostedService and its derived BackgroundService provide a framework for implementing long-running processes. Combining these with Dependency Injection (DI) allows for clean separation of concerns and better service management.

In this chapter, we explore how to integrate DI into hosted services, manage service lifetimes, and handle advanced scenarios such as multi-threaded tasks, scoped service resolution, and using Keyed Services.

Understanding Hosted Services

Hosted services in .NET are services that execute in the background while the application runs. There are two main types:

1. **IHostedService**: The base interface for defining hosted services.
2. **BackgroundService**: An abstract class that simplifies hosted service implementation.

Basic Integration of DI with Hosted Services

1. Creating a Simple Hosted Service

Example: Logging Background Service

```
public class LoggingService : BackgroundService
{
    private readonly ILogger<LoggingService> _logger;

    public LoggingService(ILogger<LoggingService> logger)
    {
        _logger = logger;
    }

    protected override async Task ExecuteAsync(CancellationToken stoppingToken)
    {
        while (!stoppingToken.IsCancellationRequested)
        {
            _logger.LogInformation($"Logging at: {DateTime.UtcNow}");
            await Task.Delay(1000, stoppingToken);
        }
    }
}
```

Registration

```
builder.Services.AddHostedService<LoggingService>();
```

2. Using Scoped Services in Hosted Services

Scoped services require special handling in background services, as their lifetime is tied to the HTTP request in web applications. To use them, create a new scope explicitly.

Example: Scoped Database Processing

```
public class DataProcessingService : BackgroundService
{
    private readonly IServiceProvider _serviceProvider;

    public DataProcessingService(IServiceProvider serviceProvider)
    {
        _serviceProvider = serviceProvider;
    }

    protected override async Task ExecuteAsync(CancellationToken stoppingToken)
    {
        while (!stoppingToken.IsCancellationRequested)
        {
            using var scope = _serviceProvider.CreateScope();
            var dbContext = scope.ServiceProvider.GetRequiredService<MyDbContext>();

            // Process data
            await dbContext.ProcessPendingDataAsync();
            await Task.Delay(5000, stoppingToken);
        }
    }
}
```

Registration

```
builder.Services.AddScoped<MyDbContext>();
builder.Services.AddHostedService<DataProcessingService>();
```

3. Handling Multi-Threaded Tasks

In multi-threaded tasks, it is essential to use thread-safe services or create separate scopes for each thread.

Example: Multi-Threaded Task Processing

```csharp
public class MultiThreadedService : BackgroundService
{
    private readonly IServiceProvider _serviceProvider;

    public MultiThreadedService(IServiceProvider serviceProvider)
    {
        _serviceProvider = serviceProvider;
    }

    protected override async Task ExecuteAsync(CancellationToken stoppingToken)
    {
        var tasks = Enumerable.Range(0, 5).Select(async _ =>
        {
            using var scope = _serviceProvider.CreateScope();
            var taskProcessor = scope.ServiceProvider.GetRequiredService<ITaskProcessor>();
            await taskProcessor.ProcessTaskAsync(stoppingToken);
        });

        await Task.WhenAll(tasks);
    }
}
```

Registration

```csharp
builder.Services.AddScoped<ITaskProcessor, TaskProcessor>();
builder.Services.AddHostedService<MultiThreadedService>();
```

Advanced Scenarios

1. Using Keyed Services in Background Tasks

Keyed Services allow dynamic resolution of services based on runtime conditions, which is particularly useful in multi-tenant or multi-environment scenarios.

Example: Multi-Tenant Background Task

```csharp
public class TenantTaskService : BackgroundService
{
    private readonly IServiceProvider _serviceProvider;

    public TenantTaskService(IServiceProvider serviceProvider)
    {
        _serviceProvider = serviceProvider;
    }

    protected override async Task ExecuteAsync(CancellationToken stoppingToken)
    {
        var tenants = new[] { "TenantA", "TenantB" };

        while (!stoppingToken.IsCancellationRequested)
        {
            foreach (var tenant in tenants)
            {
                using var scope = _serviceProvider.CreateScope();
                var tenantProcessor =
scope.ServiceProvider.GetRequiredKeyedService<ITenantProcessor>(tenant);
                await tenantProcessor.ProcessTenantDataAsync();
            }

            await Task.Delay(10000, stoppingToken);
        }
    }
}
```

Registration

```
builder.Services.AddKeyedScoped<ITenantProcessor, TenantAProcessor>("TenantA");
builder.Services.AddKeyedScoped<ITenantProcessor, TenantBProcessor>("TenantB");
builder.Services.AddHostedService<TenantTaskService>();
```

2. Combining Timers with DI

For periodic tasks, combining DI with System.Timers ensures modular, testable code.

Example: Timer-Based Background Service

```
public class TimerService : IHostedService, IDisposable
{
    private readonly IServiceProvider _serviceProvider;
    private Timer? _timer;

    public TimerService(IServiceProvider serviceProvider)
    {
        _serviceProvider = serviceProvider;
    }

    public Task StartAsync(CancellationToken cancellationToken)
    {
        _timer = new Timer(DoWork, null, TimeSpan.Zero, TimeSpan.FromSeconds(10));
        return Task.CompletedTask;
    }

    private void DoWork(object? state)
    {
        using var scope = _serviceProvider.CreateScope();
        var processor = scope.ServiceProvider.GetRequiredService<ITaskProcessor>();
        processor.ProcessTask();
```

```
    }

    public Task StopAsync(CancellationToken cancellationToken)
    {
        _timer?.Change(Timeout.Infinite, 0);
        return Task.CompletedTask;
    }

    public void Dispose()
    {
        _timer?.Dispose();
    }
}
```

Registration

```
builder.Services.AddScoped<ITaskProcessor, TaskProcessor>();
builder.Services.AddHostedService<TimerService>();
```

Testing Hosted Services

Mock dependencies and simulate the environment for testing hosted services.

Example: Testing a Hosted Service

```csharp
[Fact]
public async Task LoggingService_ShouldLogPeriodically()
{
    var loggerMock = new Mock<ILogger<LoggingService>>();
    var service = new LoggingService(loggerMock.Object);

    var cancellationTokenSource = new CancellationTokenSource();
    cancellationTokenSource.CancelAfter(3000);

    await service.StartAsync(cancellationTokenSource.Token);

    loggerMock.Verify(
        logger => logger.LogInformation(It.IsAny<string>()),
        Times.AtLeastOnce
    );
}
```

Best Practices

1. **Manage Scoped Services Carefully:**
   - Always resolve scoped services within a new scope to prevent lifetime mismatches.
2. **Leverage Keyed Services:**
   - Use Keyed Services for tenant-specific or feature-specific processing.
3. **Handle Long-Running Tasks Gracefully:**
   - Use cancellation tokens to ensure proper shutdown of tasks.
4. **Optimize Multi-Threaded Operations:**
   - Avoid shared state between threads or use thread-safe services.
5. **Test Extensively:**
   - Mock dependencies and simulate edge cases during testing.

Summary

Dependency Injection is a powerful tool for simplifying hosted services in .NET. By managing scoped services, leveraging Keyed Services, and combining DI with periodic tasks or multi-threaded operations, developers can build efficient and maintainable background processes. Following best practices ensures robust and scalable implementations.

In the next chapter, we will explore **Cross-Cutting Concerns with Dependency Injection**, focusing on how DI can simplify the implementation of concerns like logging, caching, and validation across the application.

Mastering Dependency Injection in .NET 8: Advanced Concepts and Patterns

Chapter 9: Cross-Cutting Concerns with Dependency Injection

Introduction

Cross-cutting concerns, such as logging, caching, validation, and exception handling, are functionalities that span multiple application layers. Dependency Injection (DI) in .NET simplifies the implementation of these concerns by promoting separation of concerns, reusability, and testability.

In this chapter, we will explore how to implement cross-cutting concerns using DI, including:

1. Centralized logging with DI.
2. Caching strategies.
3. Validation using middleware and services.
4. Exception handling mechanisms.
5. Advanced scenarios such as combining cross-cutting concerns with Keyed Services and dynamic resolutions.

1. Logging with DI

Centralized Logging

Example: Using ILogger with DI

```csharp
public class OrderService
{
    private readonly ILogger<OrderService> _logger;
```

```csharp
    public OrderService(ILogger<OrderService> logger)
    {
        _logger = logger;
    }

    public void ProcessOrder(int orderId)
    {
        _logger.LogInformation($"Processing order {orderId}");
        // Process logic...
        _logger.LogInformation($"Order {orderId} processed successfully");
    }
}
```

Registration

```csharp
builder.Services.AddScoped<OrderService>();
```

Combining Logging with Keyed Services

Example: Logging by Log Level

```csharp
public interface ILogHandler
{
    void Log(string message);
}

public class InfoLogHandler : ILogHandler
{
    public void Log(string message) => Console.WriteLine($"INFO: {message}");
}

public class ErrorLogHandler : ILogHandler
{
```

```csharp
    public void Log(string message) => Console.WriteLine($"ERROR: {message}");
}

public class LogProcessor
{
    private readonly IServiceProvider _serviceProvider;

    public LogProcessor(IServiceProvider serviceProvider)
    {
        _serviceProvider = serviceProvider;
    }

    public void ProcessLog(string logLevel, string message)
    {
        var handler = _serviceProvider.GetRequiredKeyedService<ILogHandler>(logLevel);
        handler.Log(message);
    }
}
```

Registration

```
builder.Services.AddKeyedSingleton<ILogHandler, InfoLogHandler>("Info");
builder.Services.AddKeyedSingleton<ILogHandler, ErrorLogHandler>("Error");
```

2. Caching with DI

Centralized Caching

Example: Using MemoryCache

```
public class ProductService
{
    private readonly IMemoryCache _cache;

    public ProductService(IMemoryCache cache)
    {
        _cache = cache;
    }

    public Product GetProduct(int productId)
    {
        if (_cache.TryGetValue(productId, out Product product))
        {
            return product;
        }

        // Simulate data fetching
        product = new Product { Id = productId, Name = "Sample Product" };
        _cache.Set(productId, product, TimeSpan.FromMinutes(5));

        return product;
    }
}
```

Registration

```
builder.Services.AddMemoryCache();
builder.Services.AddScoped<ProductService>();
```

Distributed Caching with DI

Example: Using Redis Cache

```
builder.Services.AddStackExchangeRedisCache(options =>
{
    options.Configuration = "localhost:6379";
});
```

3. Validation with DI

Validation Service

Example: Centralized Validation

```
public interface IValidator<T>
{
    void Validate(T entity);
}

public class OrderValidator : IValidator<Order>
{
    public void Validate(Order order)
    {
        if (order.TotalAmount <= 0)
            throw new ValidationException("Total amount must be greater than zero.");
    }
}
```

Usage in a Service

```
public class OrderProcessor
{
    private readonly IValidator<Order> _validator;
```

```csharp
    public OrderProcessor(IValidator<Order> validator)
    {
        _validator = validator;
    }

    public void ProcessOrder(Order order)
    {
        _validator.Validate(order);
        // Processing logic...
    }
}
```

Registration

```csharp
builder.Services.AddScoped<IValidator<Order>, OrderValidator>();
```

Middleware-Based Validation

Example: Validation Middleware

```csharp
public class ValidationMiddleware
{
    private readonly RequestDelegate _next;

    public ValidationMiddleware(RequestDelegate next)
    {
        _next = next;
    }

    public async Task InvokeAsync(HttpContext context, IValidator<HttpRequest> validator)
    {
        validator.Validate(context.Request);
        await _next(context);
    }
```

}

4. Exception Handling

Centralized Exception Logging

Example: Exception Handler Middleware

```
public class ExceptionHandlerMiddleware
{
    private readonly RequestDelegate _next;
    private readonly ILogger<ExceptionHandlerMiddleware> _logger;

    public ExceptionHandlerMiddleware(RequestDelegate next,
ILogger<ExceptionHandlerMiddleware> logger)
    {
        _next = next;
        _logger = logger;
    }

    public async Task InvokeAsync(HttpContext context)
    {
        try
        {
            await _next(context);
        }
        catch (Exception ex)
        {
            _logger.LogError($"An error occurred: {ex.Message}");
            context.Response.StatusCode = 500;
            await context.Response.WriteAsync("An internal server error occurred.");
        }
    }
}
```

Registration

```csharp
app.UseMiddleware<ExceptionHandlerMiddleware>();
```

Advanced Scenarios

Combining Cross-Cutting Concerns

Example: Logging and Validation Pipeline

```csharp
public class PipelineProcessor
{
    private readonly IValidator<Order> _validator;
    private readonly ILogger<PipelineProcessor> _logger;

    public PipelineProcessor(IValidator<Order> validator,
ILogger<PipelineProcessor> logger)
    {
        _validator = validator;
        _logger = logger;
    }

    public void ProcessOrder(Order order)
    {
        _logger.LogInformation($"Validating order {order.Id}");
        _validator.Validate(order);
        _logger.LogInformation($"Order {order.Id} validated successfully");
    }
}
```

Cross-Cutting Concerns with Keyed Services

Example: Multi-Context Validation

```
public interface IContextValidator
{
    void Validate(HttpContext context);
}

public class ApiContextValidator : IContextValidator
{
    public void Validate(HttpContext context)
    {
        if (!context.Request.Headers.ContainsKey("ApiKey"))
            throw new ValidationException("Missing API key.");
    }
}

public class WebContextValidator : IContextValidator
{
    public void Validate(HttpContext context)
    {
        if (!context.Request.Cookies.ContainsKey("SessionId"))
            throw new ValidationException("Missing session cookie.");
    }
}

builder.Services.AddKeyedSingleton<IContextValidator, ApiContextValidator>("API");
builder.Services.AddKeyedSingleton<IContextValidator, WebContextValidator>("Web");
```

Middleware

```
public class ContextValidationMiddleware
{
    private readonly RequestDelegate _next;
    private readonly IServiceProvider _serviceProvider;
```

```csharp
    public ContextValidationMiddleware(RequestDelegate next, IServiceProvider serviceProvider)
    {
        _next = next;
        _serviceProvider = serviceProvider;
    }

    public async Task InvokeAsync(HttpContext context)
    {
        var validatorKey = context.Request.Path.StartsWithSegments("/api") ? "API" : "Web";
        var validator = _serviceProvider.GetRequiredKeyedService<IContextValidator>(validatorKey);

        validator.Validate(context);
        await _next(context);
    }
}
```

Best Practices

1. **Centralize Cross-Cutting Logic:**
   - Use DI to keep cross-cutting concerns reusable and centralized.
2. **Combine Concerns Thoughtfully:**
   - Ensure that logging, validation, and caching logic does not conflict or duplicate effort.
3. **Leverage Keyed Services:**
   - Dynamically resolve context-specific implementations for flexibility.
4. **Test Concerns Separately:**
   - Mock dependencies to validate individual components.

Summary

Dependency Injection is a powerful tool for implementing cross-cutting concerns in a modular and reusable way. By leveraging DI for logging, caching, validation, and exception handling, developers can simplify application design and improve maintainability. Advanced scenarios, such as multi-context validation and dynamic resolution with Keyed Services, further extend the flexibility of these implementations.

In the next chapter, we'll explore **Dynamic Dependency Resolution with Advanced Scenarios**, focusing on runtime service selection and custom service providers.

Mastering Dependency Injection in .NET 8: Advanced Concepts and Patterns

Chapter 10: Dynamic Dependency Resolution with Advanced Scenarios

Introduction

Dynamic Dependency Resolution allows applications to select and resolve services at runtime based on contextual conditions such as user input, configuration, or environmental variables. .NET's Dependency Injection (DI) framework provides several mechanisms for implementing dynamic resolution, including IServiceProvider, Keyed Services, and custom service providers.

In this chapter, we'll explore advanced scenarios of dynamic dependency resolution, focusing on:

1. Dynamic service selection using IServiceProvider.
2. Keyed Services for multi-context resolution.
3. Runtime service registration.
4. Custom service provider implementations.
5. Real-world use cases such as multi-tenant applications, feature toggles, and dynamic middleware.

1. Dynamic Resolution with IServiceProvider

Example: Resolving Services Dynamically

```
public class DynamicServiceResolver
{
    private readonly IServiceProvider _serviceProvider;
```

```csharp
    public DynamicServiceResolver(IServiceProvider serviceProvider)
    {
        _serviceProvider = serviceProvider;
    }

    public void ResolveAndExecute(string serviceType)
    {
        var service = serviceType switch
        {
            "Email" => _serviceProvider.GetRequiredService<IEmailService>(),
            "Sms" => _serviceProvider.GetRequiredService<ISmsService>(),
            _ => throw new InvalidOperationException("Unsupported service type")
        };

        service.Execute();
    }
}
```

Registration

```csharp
builder.Services.AddScoped<IEmailService, EmailService>();
builder.Services.AddScoped<ISmsService, SmsService>();
builder.Services.AddScoped<DynamicServiceResolver>();
```

Usage

```csharp
var resolver = app.Services.GetRequiredService<DynamicServiceResolver>();
resolver.ResolveAndExecute("Email");
```

2. Using Keyed Services for Dynamic Resolution

Keyed Services simplify dynamic resolution by associating services with unique keys.

Example: Resolving Notification Services by Key

```csharp
public class NotificationProcessor
{
    private readonly IServiceProvider _serviceProvider;

    public NotificationProcessor(IServiceProvider serviceProvider)
    {
        _serviceProvider = serviceProvider;
    }

    public void ProcessNotification(string notificationType)
    {
        var service =
_serviceProvider.GetRequiredKeyedService<INotificationService>(notificationType);
        service.SendNotification("Hello, World!");
    }
}
```

Registration

```csharp
builder.Services.AddKeyedSingleton<INotificationService,
EmailNotificationService>("Email");
```

```
builder.Services.AddKeyedSingleton<INotificationService,
SmsNotificationService>("Sms");
builder.Services.AddScoped<NotificationProcessor>();
```

3. Runtime Service Registration

Dynamic scenarios often require services to be registered or updated at runtime. The IServiceCollection can be extended dynamically, but this requires careful handling.

Example: Adding Services Dynamically

```
public class DynamicRegistration
{
    private readonly IServiceCollection _services;

    public DynamicRegistration(IServiceCollection services)
    {
        _services = services;
    }

    public void RegisterService(string serviceType, Type implementationType)
    {
        _services.AddSingleton(typeof(IService), implementationType);
    }
}
```

4. Custom Service Providers

In advanced scenarios, implementing a custom service provider can provide fine-grained control over service resolution.

Example: Custom Service Provider

```csharp
public class CustomServiceProvider : IServiceProvider
{
    private readonly Dictionary<Type, Func<object>> _serviceFactories;

    public CustomServiceProvider(Dictionary<Type, Func<object>> serviceFactories)
    {
        _serviceFactories = serviceFactories;
    }

    public object GetService(Type serviceType)
    {
        return _serviceFactories.TryGetValue(serviceType, out var factory)
            ? factory()
            : throw new InvalidOperationException("Service not found");
    }
}
```

Usage

```csharp
var customProvider = new CustomServiceProvider(new Dictionary<Type, Func<object>>
{
    { typeof(IEmailService), () => new EmailService() },
    { typeof(ISmsService), () => new SmsService() }
});
var emailService = (IEmailService)customProvider.GetService(typeof(IEmailService));
emailService.Execute();
```

5. Real-World Use Cases

Multi-Tenant Applications

Resolve tenant-specific services dynamically based on request headers or context.

Example: Multi-Tenant Service Resolution

```
public class MultiTenantServiceResolver
{
    private readonly IServiceProvider _serviceProvider;

    public MultiTenantServiceResolver(IServiceProvider serviceProvider)
    {
        _serviceProvider = serviceProvider;
    }

    public ITenantService ResolveTenantService(string tenantId)
    {
        return _serviceProvider.GetRequiredKeyedService<ITenantService>(tenantId);
    }
}
```

Registration

```
builder.Services.AddKeyedSingleton<ITenantService, TenantAService>("TenantA");
builder.Services.AddKeyedSingleton<ITenantService, TenantBService>("TenantB");
builder.Services.AddScoped<MultiTenantServiceResolver>();
```

Feature Toggles

Dynamically enable or disable features using feature flags.

Example: Feature Toggle with Dynamic Resolution

```
public class FeatureService
```

```csharp
{
    private readonly IServiceProvider _serviceProvider;
    private readonly IConfiguration _configuration;

    public FeatureService(IServiceProvider serviceProvider, IConfiguration configuration)
    {
        _serviceProvider = serviceProvider;
        _configuration = configuration;
    }

    public void ExecuteFeature(string featureName)
    {
        var isEnabled = _configuration.GetValue<bool>($"Features:{featureName}");
        if (!isEnabled)
        {
            Console.WriteLine($"{featureName} is disabled.");
            return;
        }

        var feature = _serviceProvider.GetRequiredKeyedService<IFeature>(featureName);
        feature.Execute();
    }
}
```

Registration

```csharp
builder.Services.AddKeyedSingleton<IFeature, FeatureX>("FeatureX");
builder.Services.AddKeyedSingleton<IFeature, FeatureY>("FeatureY");
```

Dynamic Middleware

Inject and resolve middleware dynamically based on runtime conditions.

Example: Dynamic Middleware Resolution

```csharp
public class DynamicMiddleware
{
    private readonly RequestDelegate _next;
    private readonly IServiceProvider _serviceProvider;

    public DynamicMiddleware(RequestDelegate next, IServiceProvider serviceProvider)
    {
        _next = next;
        _serviceProvider = serviceProvider;
    }

    public async Task InvokeAsync(HttpContext context)
    {
        var middlewareType = context.Request.Headers["Middleware-Type"];
        var middleware = _serviceProvider.GetRequiredKeyedService<IMiddleware>(middlewareType);
        await middleware.InvokeAsync(context, _next);
    }
}
```

Best Practices

1. **Avoid Overusing Dynamic Resolution:**
   - Use it sparingly to avoid unnecessary complexity.
2. **Cache Resolved Services:**
   - Cache services if they are resolved frequently to improve performance.
3. **Centralize Logic:**
   - Use factories or service locators to centralize dynamic resolution logic.
4. **Handle Missing Services Gracefully:**
   - Implement fallback mechanisms for missing or unsupported services.

Summary

Dynamic Dependency Resolution provides unparalleled flexibility for real-time service selection and customization. By leveraging features like IServiceProvider, Keyed Services, runtime registration, and custom service providers, developers can build highly adaptable applications. Advanced scenarios such as multi-tenancy, feature toggles, and dynamic middleware further demonstrate the power of dynamic resolution in .NET applications.

In the next chapter, we'll explore **Performance Optimization and Debugging in Dependency Injection**, focusing on techniques to improve performance, identify bottlenecks, and debug DI-related issues effectively.

Mastering Dependency Injection in .NET 8: Advanced Concepts and Patterns

Chapter 11: Performance Optimization and Debugging in Dependency Injection

Introduction

Dependency Injection (DI) simplifies application architecture, but it can introduce performance overhead and debugging challenges, especially in large-scale systems. Optimizing DI for performance and understanding how to debug DI-related issues are crucial for building efficient and maintainable applications.

In this chapter, we'll explore:

1. Performance considerations in DI.
2. Optimizing service registration and resolution.
3. Debugging DI-related issues.
4. Tools and techniques for analyzing DI performance.
5. Real-world examples of identifying and resolving common DI problems.

1. Performance Considerations in DI

1.1 Service Resolution Overhead

Every time a service is resolved, the DI container performs checks to locate and instantiate the required dependencies. This can become a bottleneck in applications with frequent resolutions.

1.2 Large Object Graphs

Applications with deep dependency trees can experience delays during service resolution as the DI container traverses the graph.

1.3 Improper Service Lifetimes

Incorrect lifetimes, such as excessive use of Singleton or Transient, can lead to memory bloat, excessive object creation, or thread safety issues.

2. Optimizing Service Registration and Resolution

2.1 Minimize Use of Transient Services

Use Transient services only for lightweight, stateless operations.

Example: Replace Transient with Scoped Where Appropriate

```
builder.Services.AddScoped<IEmailService, EmailService>();
```

2.2 Use Factories for Expensive Objects

Avoid resolving expensive objects directly; use factories to control their lifecycle.

Example: Object Factory for Expensive Service

```
public class ExpensiveServiceFactory
{
    private readonly IServiceProvider _serviceProvider;
```

```
    public ExpensiveServiceFactory(IServiceProvider serviceProvider)
    {
        _serviceProvider = serviceProvider;
    }

    public IExpensiveService Create()
    {
        return _serviceProvider.GetRequiredService<ExpensiveService>();
    }
}
```

Registration

```
builder.Services.AddScoped<ExpensiveService>();
builder.Services.AddScoped<ExpensiveServiceFactory>();
```

2.3 Precompute Dependencies

Avoid resolving dependencies repeatedly; compute them once and reuse where possible.

Example: Caching Precomputed Dependencies

```
public class CachedService
{
    private readonly IHeavyService _cachedService;

    public CachedService(IServiceProvider serviceProvider)
    {
        _cachedService = serviceProvider.GetRequiredService<IHeavyService>();
    }
```

```csharp
    public void UseCachedService()
    {
        _cachedService.DoWork();
    }
}
```

2.4 Register Services Explicitly

Avoid scanning assemblies for automatic registration; instead, register services explicitly for better performance.

Example: Explicit Registration

```csharp
builder.Services.AddScoped<IEmailService, EmailService>();
builder.Services.AddScoped<ISmsService, SmsService>();
```

3. Debugging DI-Related Issues

3.1 Common Issues

1. **Circular Dependencies:**
   - Occurs when two or more services depend on each other directly or indirectly.

Example of Circular Dependency

```csharp
public class ServiceA
{
    public ServiceA(ServiceB serviceB) { }
```

```
}

public class ServiceB
{
    public ServiceB(ServiceA serviceA) { }
}
```

Solution

- Refactor dependencies to break the circular reference or use a factory pattern.

3.2 Service Not Registered

Occurs when attempting to resolve a service that hasn't been registered.

Solution

- Ensure all required services are registered in the IServiceCollection.

3.3 Lifetime Mismatch

Occurs when a transient or scoped service is injected into a singleton, causing runtime errors.

Solution

- Use IServiceProvider to resolve scoped or transient services within their appropriate context.

4. Tools and Techniques for Analyzing DI Performance

4.1 Built-in Logging

Enable DI container logging to capture detailed information about service registration and resolution.

Enable Logging in .NET

```
builder.Logging.AddConsole();
builder.Services.AddLogging();
```

4.2 Diagnostic Tools

1. **Dotnet Trace**
   - Use dotnet-trace to analyze DI container performance.

dotnet-trace collect --process-id <PID>

2.
3. **Application Insights**
   - Monitor DI performance in Azure using Application Insights.

4.3 Profiling Tools

Use tools like **Visual Studio Profiler** or **PerfView** to identify performance bottlenecks in DI-related code.

5. Real-World Examples

5.1 Debugging a Circular Dependency

1. **Error Message:**
   - System.InvalidOperationException: A circular dependency was detected for the service of type ServiceA.
2. **Refactor Example**
   - Break circular dependency by introducing an intermediary interface:

```
public interface IServiceResolver
{
    ServiceB GetServiceB();
}

public class ServiceResolver : IServiceResolver
{
    private readonly IServiceProvider _serviceProvider;

    public ServiceResolver(IServiceProvider serviceProvider)
    {
        _serviceProvider = serviceProvider;
    }

    public ServiceB GetServiceB()
    {
        return _serviceProvider.GetRequiredService<ServiceB>();
    }
}
```

5.2 Resolving a Performance Bottleneck

1. **Scenario:**
   - Slow service resolution due to repeated creation of a transient service.
2. **Solution:**
   - Cache the service instance:

```csharp
public class CachedTransientService
{
    private readonly IServiceProvider _serviceProvider;
    private IHeavyService? _cachedService;

    public CachedTransientService(IServiceProvider serviceProvider)
    {
        _serviceProvider = serviceProvider;
    }

    public IHeavyService GetService()
    {
        return _cachedService ??= _serviceProvider.GetRequiredService<IHeavyService>();
    }
}
```

Best Practices

1. **Analyze Service Lifetimes:**
   - Choose appropriate lifetimes (Singleton, Scoped, Transient) based on use cases.
2. **Avoid Overuse of Transient:**
   - Use Transient only when a new instance is essential.

3. **Enable DI Logging:**
   - Use logging to diagnose issues early during development.
4. **Test Performance Regularly:**
   - Benchmark critical DI components using tools like BenchmarkDotNet.
5. **Refactor Circular Dependencies:**
   - Break circular dependencies with factory patterns or intermediary services.

Summary

Optimizing Dependency Injection involves careful management of service lifetimes, caching strategies, and dynamic resolution. Debugging DI-related issues, such as circular dependencies and lifetime mismatches, requires a deep understanding of the DI container and effective use of diagnostic tools. By following best practices and leveraging tools, developers can build efficient and scalable applications.

In the next chapter, we will explore **Designing Modular and Extensible Applications with Dependency Injection**, focusing on how DI promotes modularity, extensibility, and maintainability in large-scale systems.

Chapter 12: Designing Modular and Extensible Applications with Dependency Injection

Introduction

Modular and extensible application design is essential for scalability, maintainability, and adaptability to changing requirements. Dependency Injection (DI) plays a pivotal role in achieving modularity by decoupling components, promoting reusability, and simplifying integration.

In this chapter, we explore:

1. Key principles of modular and extensible design.
2. Leveraging DI for modularity.
3. Extending applications dynamically with DI.
4. Real-world architectural patterns like plugins, microservices, and feature modules.
5. Advanced DI techniques for maintaining loose coupling.

1. Principles of Modular and Extensible Design

1. **Separation of Concerns:**
    - Each module should focus on a specific functionality.
    - Example: Separate user authentication from data processing.
2. **Low Coupling, High Cohesion:**

- Modules should have minimal dependencies between each other but work cohesively within themselves.
3. **Open-Closed Principle:**
    - Modules should be open for extension but closed for modification.
4. **Plug-and-Play Architecture:**
    - Modules should be replaceable or upgradable without impacting other components.

2. Leveraging DI for Modularity

Dependency Injection facilitates modular design by:

1. Allowing dynamic replacement of components.
2. Centralizing service registration.
3. Supporting runtime service selection.

Example: Modular User Management System

Step 1: Define Interfaces for Modules

```
public interface IUserService
{
    void CreateUser(string name);
}

public interface IRoleService
{
    void AssignRole(string user, string role);
}
```

Step 2: Implement the Modules

```csharp
public class UserService : IUserService
{
    public void CreateUser(string name)
    {
        Console.WriteLine($"User {name} created.");
    }
}

public class RoleService : IRoleService
{
    public void AssignRole(string user, string role)
    {
        Console.WriteLine($"Role {role} assigned to {user}.");
    }
}
```

Step 3: Register Modules in DI Container

```csharp
builder.Services.AddScoped<IUserService, UserService>();
builder.Services.AddScoped<IRoleService, RoleService>();
```

Step 4: Inject and Use Modules

```csharp
public class AccountManager
{
    private readonly IUserService _userService;
    private readonly IRoleService _roleService;

    public AccountManager(IUserService userService, IRoleService roleService)
    {
        _userService = userService;
        _roleService = roleService;
    }

    public void ManageAccount(string name, string role)
```

```
    {
        _userService.CreateUser(name);
        _roleService.AssignRole(name, role);
    }
}
```

3. Extending Applications Dynamically with DI

Example: Adding Plugins at Runtime

Step 1: Define a Plugin Interface

```
public interface IPlugin
{
    void Execute();
}
```

Step 2: Implement Plugins

```
public class EmailPlugin : IPlugin
{
    public void Execute()
    {
        Console.WriteLine("Executing Email Plugin.");
    }
}

public class SmsPlugin : IPlugin
{
    public void Execute()
    {
        Console.WriteLine("Executing SMS Plugin.");
    }
}
```

Step 3: Register Plugins Dynamically

```
var plugins = new List<Type> { typeof(EmailPlugin), typeof(SmsPlugin) };

foreach (var plugin in plugins)
{
    builder.Services.AddSingleton(typeof(IPlugin), plugin);
}
```

Step 4: Resolve and Execute Plugins

```
var pluginServices = app.Services.GetServices<IPlugin>();
foreach (var plugin in pluginServices)
{
    plugin.Execute();
}
```

4. Real-World Architectural Patterns

4.1 Plugin Architecture

Use DI to load and manage plugins dynamically, enabling extensibility without modifying the core application.

Example: Dynamic Plugin Manager

```
public class PluginManager
{
    private readonly IEnumerable<IPlugin> _plugins;

    public PluginManager(IEnumerable<IPlugin> plugins)
    {
        _plugins = plugins;
    }
```

```csharp
    public void ExecutePlugins()
    {
        foreach (var plugin in _plugins)
        {
            plugin.Execute();
        }
    }
}
```

4.2 Microservices

DI simplifies microservice architecture by decoupling service implementations and enabling dynamic service discovery.

Example: Service Locator for Microservices

```csharp
public class MicroserviceLocator
{
    private readonly IServiceProvider _serviceProvider;

    public MicroserviceLocator(IServiceProvider serviceProvider)
    {
        _serviceProvider = serviceProvider;
    }

    public T GetService<T>(string serviceName)
    {
        return _serviceProvider.GetRequiredKeyedService<T>(serviceName);
    }
}
```

Registration

```csharp
builder.Services.AddKeyedSingleton<IOrderService, OrderService>("OrderService");
builder.Services.AddKeyedSingleton<IPaymentService, PaymentService>("PaymentService");
```

4.3 Feature Modules

Feature modules allow modular development and deployment of application features.

Example: Feature Module for Reporting

```csharp
public interface IReportService
{
    void GenerateReport();
}

public class PdfReportService : IReportService
{
    public void GenerateReport()
    {
        Console.WriteLine("PDF report generated.");
    }
}

public class ExcelReportService : IReportService
{
    public void GenerateReport()
    {
        Console.WriteLine("Excel report generated.");
    }
}

builder.Services.AddScoped<IReportService, PdfReportService>();
```

5. Advanced DI Techniques for Loose Coupling

5.1 Using Factories for Modular Dependencies

```csharp
public class ServiceFactory
{
    private readonly IServiceProvider _serviceProvider;

    public ServiceFactory(IServiceProvider serviceProvider)
    {
        _serviceProvider = serviceProvider;
    }

    public T CreateService<T>()
    {
        return _serviceProvider.GetRequiredService<T>();
    }
}
```

5.2 Dynamic Resolution for Feature Toggles

```csharp
public class FeatureToggleService
{
    private readonly IServiceProvider _serviceProvider;

    public FeatureToggleService(IServiceProvider serviceProvider)
    {
        _serviceProvider = serviceProvider;
    }

    public void ExecuteFeature(string featureName)
    {
        var feature =
_serviceProvider.GetRequiredKeyedService<IFeature>(featureName);
        feature.Execute();
    }
```

}

Best Practices

1. **Design for Extensibility:**
   - Use interfaces and DI to abstract module implementations.
2. **Centralize Service Registration:**
   - Maintain a single point for registering services.
3. **Use Keyed Services for Modularity:**
   - Dynamically resolve services based on runtime context or configuration.
4. **Promote Reusability:**
   - Ensure modules are self-contained and reusable across applications.
5. **Test Modular Components Independently:**
   - Use dependency mocks to test individual modules.

Summary

Dependency Injection is a powerful enabler of modular and extensible application design. By leveraging DI to decouple components, dynamically resolve services, and manage plugins or feature modules, developers can build scalable and maintainable systems. Advanced DI techniques, such as factories and dynamic resolution, further enhance flexibility and adaptability.

In the next chapter, we will explore **Integrating Dependency Injection in Cross-Platform Applications**, focusing on leveraging DI in mobile, desktop, and cloud-native applications.

Chapter 13: Integrating Dependency Injection in Cross-Platform Applications

Introduction

Modern software development increasingly demands cross-platform solutions that run on mobile, desktop, and cloud environments. Dependency Injection (DI) is critical for ensuring consistency, maintainability, and flexibility across these platforms. .NET's built-in DI framework makes it easy to manage shared dependencies and platform-specific services.

In this chapter, we explore:

1. Integrating DI in mobile applications using **Xamarin** and **.NET MAUI**.
2. Using DI in desktop applications with **WPF** and **WinForms**.
3. Cloud-native DI strategies for Azure and AWS.
4. Best practices for cross-platform dependency management.
5. Advanced techniques for platform-specific service resolution.

1. DI in Mobile Applications

1.1 Dependency Injection in Xamarin and .NET MAUI

Example: DI in a .NET MAUI Application

Step 1: Create Shared Services

```csharp
public interface IDataService
{
    string GetData();
}

public class DataService : IDataService
{
    public string GetData() => "Hello from DataService!";
}
```

Step 2: Register Services

```csharp
public static class MauiProgram
{
    public static MauiApp CreateMauiApp()
    {
        var builder = MauiApp.CreateBuilder();

        builder.Services.AddSingleton<IDataService, DataService>();

        return builder.Build();
    }
}
```

Step 3: Use DI in Pages

```csharp
public partial class MainPage : ContentPage
{
    private readonly IDataService _dataService;

    public MainPage(IDataService dataService)
    {
        InitializeComponent();
        _dataService = dataService;
        Label.Text = _dataService.GetData();
    }
}
```

1.2 Platform-Specific Implementations

Example: Platform-Specific Service

```csharp
public interface IPlatformService
{
    string GetPlatformName();
}

public class AndroidPlatformService : IPlatformService
{
    public string GetPlatformName() => "Android";
}

public class iOSPlatformService : IPlatformService
{
    public string GetPlatformName() => "iOS";
}

}
```

Registration

```csharp
#if ANDROID
builder.Services.AddSingleton<IPlatformService, AndroidPlatformService>();
#elif IOS
builder.Services.AddSingleton<IPlatformService, iOSPlatformService>();
#endif
```

2. DI in Desktop Applications

2.1 Using DI in WPF

Example: WPF with DI

Step 1: Configure Services in App.xaml.cs

```
public partial class App : Application
{
    public IServiceProvider ServiceProvider { get; private set; }

    protected override void OnStartup(StartupEventArgs e)
    {
        var serviceCollection = new ServiceCollection();
        ConfigureServices(serviceCollection);

        ServiceProvider = serviceCollection.BuildServiceProvider();

        var mainWindow = ServiceProvider.GetRequiredService<MainWindow>();
        mainWindow.Show();
    }

    private void ConfigureServices(IServiceCollection services)
    {
        services.AddSingleton<IDataService, DataService>();
        services.AddSingleton<MainWindow>();
    }
}
```

Step 2: Inject Services in MainWindow

```
public partial class MainWindow : Window
{
    private readonly IDataService _dataService;

    public MainWindow(IDataService dataService)
    {
        InitializeComponent();
```

```
        _dataService = dataService;
        Label.Content = _dataService.GetData();
    }
}
```

2.2 Using DI in WinForms

Example: WinForms with DI

Step 1: Configure Services in Program.cs

```
public static class Program
{
    public static IServiceProvider ServiceProvider { get; private set; }

    [STAThread]
    static void Main()
    {
        ApplicationConfiguration.Initialize();

        var services = new ServiceCollection();
        ConfigureServices(services);

        ServiceProvider = services.BuildServiceProvider();
        Application.Run(ServiceProvider.GetRequiredService<MainForm>());
    }

    private static void ConfigureServices(IServiceCollection services)
    {
        services.AddSingleton<IDataService, DataService>();
        services.AddSingleton<MainForm>();
    }
}
```

Step 2: Inject Services in MainForm

```
public partial class MainForm : Form
{
    private readonly IDataService _dataService;

    public MainForm(IDataService dataService)
    {
        InitializeComponent();
        label.Text = _dataService.GetData();
    }
}
```

3. DI in Cloud-Native Applications

3.1 Azure Functions

DI in Azure Functions simplifies managing shared services and configurations.

Example: Azure Function with DI

Step 1: Register Services in Startup

```
[assembly: FunctionsStartup(typeof(MyFunctionApp.Startup))]

public class Startup : FunctionsStartup
{
    public override void Configure(IFunctionsHostBuilder builder)
    {
        builder.Services.AddSingleton<IDataService, DataService>();
    }
}
```

Step 2: Inject Services in Function

```
public class MyFunction
```

```csharp
{
    private readonly IDataService _dataService;

    public MyFunction(IDataService dataService)
    {
        _dataService = dataService;
    }

    [FunctionName("MyFunction")]
    public IActionResult Run([HttpTrigger(AuthorizationLevel.Function, "get")] HttpRequest req)
    {
        return new OkObjectResult(_dataService.GetData());
    }
}
```

3.2 AWS Lambda

Use DI in AWS Lambda functions for shared service resolution.

Example: AWS Lambda with DI

Step 1: Configure DI in Startup

```csharp
public class Startup
{
    public static IServiceProvider BuildServiceProvider()
    {
        var services = new ServiceCollection();
        services.AddSingleton<IDataService, DataService>();
        return services.BuildServiceProvider();
    }
}
```

Step 2: Inject Services in Lambda Handler

```
public class LambdaFunction
{
    private readonly IDataService _dataService;

    public LambdaFunction()
    {
        var serviceProvider = Startup.BuildServiceProvider();
        _dataService = serviceProvider.GetRequiredService<IDataService>();
    }

    public string FunctionHandler()
    {
        return _dataService.GetData();
    }
}
```

4. Best Practices for Cross-Platform Dependency Management

1. **Abstract Shared Logic:**
   - Define common interfaces for shared services.
   - Implement platform-specific logic only when necessary.
2. **Leverage Conditional Compilation:**
   - Use #if directives to register platform-specific implementations.
3. **Centralize DI Configuration:**
   - Maintain a single entry point for service registration.
4. **Test Across Platforms:**
   - Mock dependencies to validate functionality independently for each platform.
5. **Minimize Platform-Specific Code:**
   - Keep platform-specific implementations isolated and minimal.

5. Advanced Techniques for Platform-Specific Resolution

Using Factories for Platform-Specific Services

```csharp
public class PlatformServiceFactory
{
    private readonly IServiceProvider _serviceProvider;

    public PlatformServiceFactory(IServiceProvider serviceProvider)
    {
        _serviceProvider = serviceProvider;
    }

    public IPlatformService GetService()
    {
#if ANDROID
        return _serviceProvider.GetRequiredService<AndroidPlatformService>();
#elif IOS
        return _serviceProvider.GetRequiredService<iOSPlatformService>();
#else
        throw new NotSupportedException("Platform not supported");
#endif
    }
}
```

Summary

Dependency Injection ensures modularity, reusability, and consistency across platforms. By leveraging DI in mobile, desktop, and cloud-native applications, developers can build scalable and maintainable cross-platform solutions. Advanced techniques like platform-specific service resolution and centralized DI configuration further enhance development efficiency.

In the next chapter, we will explore **Testing and Mocking with Dependency Injection**, focusing on strategies to test DI-integrated components and mock services effectively.

Chapter 14: EF Core for Service Factory in Background Services

Introduction

Background services often require interaction with databases for operations like data processing, reporting, or cleanup tasks. Using **Entity Framework (EF) Core** with a Service Factory ensures efficient, scoped management of database contexts and dependencies in long-running background services.

This chapter explores:

1. Leveraging EF Core in background services.
2. Using a Service Factory for database context management.
3. Real-world examples of processing tasks with EF Core.
4. Best practices for managing EF Core and DI in background services.

1. Leveraging EF Core in Background Services

Challenges

1. **Scoped Context Management:**
    - EF Core DbContext instances must be scoped per request or operation.
2. **Thread Safety:**
    - Background services often involve multi-threaded operations that require thread-safe handling of DbContext.

Solution

- Use **Service Factories** to create scoped instances of DbContext dynamically.

---

2. Implementing a Service Factory for EF Core

Step 1: Define a Factory Interface

```
public interface IDbContextFactory
{
    MyDbContext CreateDbContext();
}
```

Step 2: Implement the Factory

```
public class DbContextFactory : IDbContextFactory
{
    private readonly IServiceProvider _serviceProvider;

    public DbContextFactory(IServiceProvider serviceProvider)
    {
        _serviceProvider = serviceProvider;
    }

    public MyDbContext CreateDbContext()
    {
        return _serviceProvider.GetRequiredService<MyDbContext>();
    }
}
```

Step 3: Register the Factory

```
builder.Services.AddDbContext<MyDbContext>(options =>
    options.UseSqlServer("YourConnectionString"));
builder.Services.AddSingleton<IDbContextFactory, DbContextFactory>();
```

3. Using EF Core in a Background Service

Example: Background Service for Data Processing

Step 1: Implement the Background Service

```csharp
public class DataProcessingService : BackgroundService
{
    private readonly IDbContextFactory _dbContextFactory;

    public DataProcessingService(IDbContextFactory dbContextFactory)
    {
        _dbContextFactory = dbContextFactory;
    }

    protected override async Task ExecuteAsync(CancellationToken stoppingToken)
    {
        while (!stoppingToken.IsCancellationRequested)
        {
            using var dbContext = _dbContextFactory.CreateDbContext();

            // Fetch and process data
            var pendingItems = await dbContext.Items
                .Where(item => item.Status == "Pending")
                .ToListAsync(stoppingToken);

            foreach (var item in pendingItems)
            {
                item.Status = "Processed";
                dbContext.Update(item);
            }

            await dbContext.SaveChangesAsync(stoppingToken);
```

```
            await Task.Delay(5000, stoppingToken); // Pause before next iteration
        }
    }
}
```

Step 2: Register the Background Service

```
builder.Services.AddHostedService<DataProcessingService>();
```

4. Advanced Scenarios

4.1 Multi-Tenant Database Operations

For multi-tenant systems, resolve DbContext configurations dynamically based on tenant identifiers.

Example: Tenant-Specific DbContext

```
public class TenantDbContextFactory : IDbContextFactory
{
    private readonly IServiceProvider _serviceProvider;

    public TenantDbContextFactory(IServiceProvider serviceProvider)
    {
        _serviceProvider = serviceProvider;
    }

    public MyDbContext CreateDbContext(string tenantId)
    {
        var options = new DbContextOptionsBuilder<MyDbContext>()
            .UseSqlServer($"YourConnectionString_{tenantId}")
            .Options;

        return new MyDbContext(options);
    }
```

}

Usage in Background Service

```
using var dbContext = _dbContextFactory.CreateDbContext("TenantA");
```

4.2 Batch Processing

For batch processing large datasets, use EF Core's streaming capabilities to reduce memory usage.

Example: Streaming Large Datasets

```
var items = dbContext.Items.AsNoTracking().Where(item => item.Status == "Pending");

await foreach (var item in items.AsAsyncEnumerable())
{
    item.Status = "Processed";
    dbContext.Update(item);
}

await dbContext.SaveChangesAsync();
```

5. Best Practices

1. **Scoped DbContext Management:**
   - Always resolve DbContext within a new scope.
2. **Avoid Long-Lived DbContext Instances:**

- Dispose of DbContext instances after each operation to prevent memory leaks.
3. **Use Asynchronous Methods:**
    - Prefer async methods (SaveChangesAsync, ToListAsync) to avoid blocking threads.
4. **Optimize Queries:**
    - Use projections and filters (AsNoTracking, Where) to improve query performance.
5. **Monitor Performance:**
    - Profile EF Core queries using tools like Application Insights or SQL Profiler.

6. Real-World Use Case

Scenario: Automated Email Notifications

- A background service fetches unprocessed email notifications from the database, sends them, and updates their status.

Implementation

1. Fetch unprocessed notifications using EF Core.
2. Send emails using an injected email service.
3. Update the status in the database.

Code

```
protected override async Task ExecuteAsync(CancellationToken stoppingToken)
{
    while (!stoppingToken.IsCancellationRequested)
```

```csharp
{
    using var dbContext = _dbContextFactory.CreateDbContext();

    var emails = await dbContext.Emails
        .Where(email => email.Status == "Pending")
        .ToListAsync(stoppingToken);

    foreach (var email in emails)
    {
        await _emailService.SendAsync(email);
        email.Status = "Sent";
        dbContext.Update(email);
    }

    await dbContext.SaveChangesAsync(stoppingToken);
    await Task.Delay(10000, stoppingToken);
    }
}
```

Summary

Using a Service Factory with EF Core ensures efficient, thread-safe database context management in background services. This approach simplifies complex data-driven operations like batch processing, multi-tenant data management, and streaming large datasets. By following best practices, developers can build robust and scalable background services with EF Core and DI.

Chapter 15: Testing and Mocking with Dependency Injection

Introduction

Testing and mocking are integral to building reliable and maintainable applications. Dependency Injection (DI) simplifies testing by decoupling dependencies, enabling the use of mock objects, and facilitating isolated unit tests. By leveraging DI, developers can write robust tests for services, controllers, background tasks, and more.

This chapter explores:

1. Testing strategies with DI.
2. Mocking dependencies for unit and integration tests.
3. Using tools like Moq and Microsoft.Extensions.DependencyInjection for test setups.
4. Real-world examples of testing DI-based components.
5. Best practices for test-driven development (TDD) with DI.

1. Testing Strategies with DI

1.1 Unit Testing

Unit tests validate individual components in isolation. With DI, real dependencies are replaced by mocks or stubs, allowing precise control over test scenarios.

1.2 Integration Testing

Integration tests validate the interaction between multiple components. DI simplifies integration tests by enabling real dependencies while configuring the test-specific environment.

1.3 End-to-End Testing

In end-to-end tests, DI can manage a complete application environment, ensuring all dependencies are correctly initialized and interact seamlessly.

2. Mocking Dependencies for Unit Tests

2.1 Using Moq for Mocking

Example: Testing a Service with Mocked Dependency

```
public interface IDataService
{
    string GetData();
}

public class BusinessService
{
    private readonly IDataService _dataService;

    public BusinessService(IDataService dataService)
    {
        _dataService = dataService;
    }

    public string ProcessData()
    {
        var data = _dataService.GetData();
        return $"Processed: {data}";
    }
```

}

Unit Test

```csharp
[Fact]
public void ProcessData_ShouldReturnProcessedData()
{
    // Arrange
    var mockDataService = new Mock<IDataService>();
    mockDataService.Setup(ds => ds.GetData()).Returns("TestData");

    var businessService = new BusinessService(mockDataService.Object);

    // Act
    var result = businessService.ProcessData();

    // Assert
    Assert.Equal("Processed: TestData", result);
}
```

2.2 Mocking Multiple Dependencies

Example: Mocking Multiple Dependencies

```csharp
public interface IEmailService
{
    void SendEmail(string recipient, string message);
}

public class NotificationService
{
    private readonly IDataService _dataService;
    private readonly IEmailService _emailService;
```

```csharp
    public NotificationService(IDataService dataService, IEmailService emailService)
    {
        _dataService = dataService;
        _emailService = emailService;
    }

    public void Notify(string recipient)
    {
        var data = _dataService.GetData();
        _emailService.SendEmail(recipient, $"Notification: {data}");
    }
}
```

Unit Test

```csharp
[Fact]
public void Notify_ShouldSendEmailWithProcessedData()
{
    // Arrange
    var mockDataService = new Mock<IDataService>();
    var mockEmailService = new Mock<IEmailService>();

    mockDataService.Setup(ds => ds.GetData()).Returns("TestData");

    var notificationService = new NotificationService(mockDataService.Object, mockEmailService.Object);

    // Act
    notificationService.Notify("test@example.com");

    // Assert
    mockEmailService.Verify(es => es.SendEmail("test@example.com", "Notification: TestData"), Times.Once);
}
```

3. Setting Up DI for Integration Tests

3.1 Using In-Memory Databases

Example: Testing with In-Memory Database

```csharp
public class MyDbContext : DbContext
{
    public DbSet<Item> Items { get; set; }

    public MyDbContext(DbContextOptions<MyDbContext> options) : base(options) { }
}

[Fact]
public async Task AddItem_ShouldSaveToDatabase()
{
    // Arrange
    var options = new DbContextOptionsBuilder<MyDbContext>()
        .UseInMemoryDatabase("TestDb")
        .Options;

    var dbContext = new MyDbContext(options);
    dbContext.Items.Add(new Item { Name = "TestItem" });
    await dbContext.SaveChangesAsync();

    // Act
    var items = await dbContext.Items.ToListAsync();

    // Assert
    Assert.Single(items);
    Assert.Equal("TestItem", items[0].Name);
}
```

3.2 Configuring Dependency Injection for Integration Tests

Example: Custom Service Provider for Testing

```csharp
[Fact]
public async Task Service_ShouldUseRealDependencies()
{
    // Arrange
    var services = new ServiceCollection();
    services.AddDbContext<MyDbContext>(options =>
        options.UseInMemoryDatabase("TestDb"));
    services.AddScoped<IDataService, DataService>();

    var serviceProvider = services.BuildServiceProvider();

    var dataService = serviceProvider.GetRequiredService<IDataService>();

    // Act
    var result = dataService.GetData();

    // Assert
    Assert.Equal("ExpectedData", result);
}
```

4. Real-World Testing Scenarios

4.1 Testing Background Services

Example: Testing a Background Service

```csharp
public class BackgroundProcessor : BackgroundService
{
    private readonly IDataService _dataService;

    public BackgroundProcessor(IDataService dataService)
    {
        _dataService = dataService;
    }

    protected override async Task ExecuteAsync(CancellationToken stoppingToken)
    {
```

```csharp
        while (!stoppingToken.IsCancellationRequested)
        {
            _dataService.GetData();
            await Task.Delay(1000, stoppingToken);
        }
    }
}
```

Test

```csharp
[Fact]
public async Task BackgroundProcessor_ShouldCallGetDataPeriodically()
{
    // Arrange
    var mockDataService = new Mock<IDataService>();
    var service = new BackgroundProcessor(mockDataService.Object);

    var cts = new CancellationTokenSource();
    cts.CancelAfter(3000);

    // Act
    await service.StartAsync(cts.Token);

    // Assert
    mockDataService.Verify(ds => ds.GetData(), Times.AtLeastOnce);
}
```

4.2 Testing Middleware

Example: Testing Middleware

```csharp
public class LoggingMiddleware
{
    private readonly RequestDelegate _next;
```

```csharp
    private readonly ILogger<LoggingMiddleware> _logger;

    public LoggingMiddleware(RequestDelegate next, ILogger<LoggingMiddleware> logger)
    {
        _next = next;
        _logger = logger;
    }

    public async Task InvokeAsync(HttpContext context)
    {
        _logger.LogInformation($"Request Path: {context.Request.Path}");
        await _next(context);
    }
}

[Fact]
public async Task LoggingMiddleware_ShouldLogRequestPath()
{
    // Arrange
    var loggerMock = new Mock<ILogger<LoggingMiddleware>>();
    var middleware = new LoggingMiddleware(context => Task.CompletedTask, loggerMock.Object);

    var context = new DefaultHttpContext();
    context.Request.Path = "/test";

    // Act
    await middleware.InvokeAsync(context);

    // Assert
    loggerMock.Verify(logger => logger.LogInformation($"Request Path: /test"), Times.Once);
}
```

5. Best Practices

1. **Mock Dependencies:**
   - Replace real dependencies with mocks for unit tests.
2. **Use In-Memory Databases:**
   - For integration tests, simulate database operations with in-memory databases.
3. **Isolate Tests:**
   - Ensure tests do not interfere with each other by using separate environments or setups.
4. **Test Service Lifetimes:**
   - Validate correct lifetimes for services (Scoped, Singleton, Transient) in your tests.
5. **Use Test-Specific Configurations:**
   - Provide test-specific configurations or dependency overrides.

Summary

Dependency Injection enhances testing and mocking by decoupling components and enabling controlled test environments. By using tools like Moq, in-memory databases, and custom DI setups, developers can create reliable unit, integration, and end-to-end tests. Following best practices ensures high-quality and maintainable test suites.

In the next chapter, we will explore **Design Patterns with Advanced Dependency Injection**, diving into complex design patterns such as Mediator, Proxy, and Composite with DI.

Chapter 16: Design Patterns with Advanced Dependency Injection

Introduction

Design patterns provide proven solutions to recurring problems in software design. Advanced Dependency Injection (DI) in .NET simplifies the implementation of many complex design patterns, such as **Mediator**, **Proxy**, **Composite**, and more. By leveraging DI, developers can dynamically resolve dependencies, reduce boilerplate code, and create extensible, maintainable systems.

In this chapter, we'll explore:

1. Implementing the **Mediator Pattern** with DI.
2. Creating dynamic proxies using DI.
3. Managing tree-like structures with the **Composite Pattern**.
4. Using the **Decorator Pattern** for extensible behavior.
5. Real-world scenarios and best practices.

1. Mediator Pattern with DI

Overview

The Mediator Pattern centralizes communication between components to reduce dependencies and enable dynamic behavior. DI simplifies mediator implementation by dynamically resolving handlers for specific requests.

Example: Command Handling with Mediator

Step 1: Define Commands

```csharp
public interface ICommand
{
    void Execute();
}

public class CreateOrderCommand : ICommand
{
    public void Execute() => Console.WriteLine("Order created.");
}

public class CancelOrderCommand : ICommand
{
    public void Execute() => Console.WriteLine("Order canceled.");
}
```

Step 2: Implement a Mediator

```csharp
public interface IMediator
{
    void HandleCommand<TCommand>() where TCommand : ICommand;
}

public class Mediator : IMediator
{
    private readonly IServiceProvider _serviceProvider;

    public Mediator(IServiceProvider serviceProvider)
    {
        _serviceProvider = serviceProvider;
    }

    public void HandleCommand<TCommand>() where TCommand : ICommand
    {
        var command = _serviceProvider.GetRequiredService<TCommand>();
        command.Execute();
    }
}
```

Step 3: Register Services

```csharp
builder.Services.AddScoped<ICommand, CreateOrderCommand>();
builder.Services.AddScoped<ICommand, CancelOrderCommand>();
builder.Services.AddScoped<IMediator, Mediator>();
```

Step 4: Use the Mediator

```csharp
public class OrderProcessor
{
    private readonly IMediator _mediator;

    public OrderProcessor(IMediator mediator)
    {
        _mediator = mediator;
    }

    public void ProcessOrder()
    {
        _mediator.HandleCommand<CreateOrderCommand>();
        _mediator.HandleCommand<CancelOrderCommand>();
    }
}
```

2. Proxy Pattern with DI

Overview

The Proxy Pattern provides a surrogate or placeholder to control access to an object. DI enables dynamic proxy generation, reducing manual proxy creation.

Example: Authorization Proxy

Step 1: Define the Interface and Real Service

```csharp
public interface IOrderService
{
    void PlaceOrder();
```

```csharp
}

public class OrderService : IOrderService
{
    public void PlaceOrder()
    {
        Console.WriteLine("Order placed.");
    }
}
```

Step 2: Implement the Proxy

```csharp
public class AuthorizationProxy : IOrderService
{
    private readonly IOrderService _orderService;

    public AuthorizationProxy(IOrderService orderService)
    {
        _orderService = orderService;
    }

    public void PlaceOrder()
    {
        Console.WriteLine("Authorization successful.");
        _orderService.PlaceOrder();
    }
}
```

Step 3: Register the Proxy

```csharp
builder.Services.AddScoped<IOrderService, OrderService>();
builder.Services.Decorate<IOrderService, AuthorizationProxy>();
```

Step 4: Use the Proxy

```csharp
var orderService = app.Services.GetRequiredService<IOrderService>();
orderService.PlaceOrder();
```

3. Composite Pattern with DI

Mastering Dependency Injection in .NET 8: Advanced Concepts and Patterns

Overview

The Composite Pattern is useful for representing tree-like structures where a group of objects is treated as a single entity. DI simplifies the dynamic composition of these structures.

Example: Building a Menu System

Step 1: Define the Component Interface

```csharp
public interface IMenuComponent
{
    void Display();
}
```

Step 2: Implement Leaf and Composite

```csharp
public class MenuItem : IMenuComponent
{
    private readonly string _name;

    public MenuItem(string name)
    {
        _name = name;
    }

    public void Display() => Console.WriteLine($"Item: {_name}");
}

public class Menu : IMenuComponent
{
    private readonly List<IMenuComponent> _components = new();

    public void Add(IMenuComponent component)
    {
        _components.Add(component);
    }
```

```csharp
    public void Display()
    {
        foreach (var component in _components)
        {
            component.Display();
        }
    }
}
```

Step 3: Use DI to Build the Composite

```csharp
builder.Services.AddScoped<IMenuComponent>(sp =>
{
    var menu = new Menu();
    menu.Add(new MenuItem("File"));
    menu.Add(new MenuItem("Edit"));
    return menu;
});
```

Step 4: Use the Composite

```csharp
var menu = app.Services.GetRequiredService<IMenuComponent>();
menu.Display();
```

4. Decorator Pattern with DI

Overview

The Decorator Pattern allows behavior to be added to individual objects dynamically. DI supports dynamic decoration by injecting additional services.

Example: Logging Decorator

Step 1: Define the Interface and Real Service

```csharp
public interface IPaymentService
{
    void ProcessPayment();
```

```csharp
}

public class PaymentService : IPaymentService
{
    public void ProcessPayment() => Console.WriteLine("Payment processed.");
}
```

Step 2: Implement the Decorator

```csharp
public class LoggingDecorator : IPaymentService
{
    private readonly IPaymentService _paymentService;

    public LoggingDecorator(IPaymentService paymentService)
    {
        _paymentService = paymentService;
    }

    public void ProcessPayment()
    {
        Console.WriteLine("Logging: Payment processing started.");
        _paymentService.ProcessPayment();
        Console.WriteLine("Logging: Payment processing finished.");
    }
}
```

Step 3: Register the Decorator

```csharp
builder.Services.AddScoped<IPaymentService, PaymentService>();
builder.Services.Decorate<IPaymentService, LoggingDecorator>();
```

Step 4: Use the Decorator

```csharp
var paymentService = app.Services.GetRequiredService<IPaymentService>();
paymentService.ProcessPayment();
```

5. Real-World Scenarios

1. **Mediator for Event Handling:**
   - Use the Mediator Pattern for handling domain events or commands in microservices.
2. **Proxy for Security:**
   - Use the Proxy Pattern to implement logging, caching, or authorization.
3. **Composite for UI Rendering:**
   - Build tree structures for UI components like menus or dashboards.
4. **Decorator for Extensible Features:**
   - Use the Decorator Pattern to add new features like logging or validation without modifying the base class.

Best Practices

1. **Use DI to Simplify Patterns:**
   - Avoid manual dependency resolution; let the DI container handle it.
2. **Leverage Decorators for Cross-Cutting Concerns:**
   - Use decorators to implement features like logging, validation, or caching.
3. **Keep Components Independent:**
   - Ensure components adhere to the single responsibility principle.
4. **Test Patterns in Isolation:**
   - Mock dependencies to test individual patterns independently.
5. **Combine Patterns for Complex Scenarios:**
   - Use multiple patterns (e.g., Mediator + Decorator) to handle advanced use cases.

Summary

Advanced Dependency Injection simplifies the implementation of complex design patterns like Mediator, Proxy, Composite, and Decorator. These patterns help developers build flexible, modular, and maintainable systems. By leveraging DI, developers can dynamically resolve dependencies, add extensibility, and manage component lifetimes effectively.

In the next chapter, we will explore **Future Trends in Dependency Injection**, focusing on emerging features, best practices, and the evolution of DI in modern software development.

Chapter 17: Advanced Techniques with Dependency Injection - Service Decoration and Dynamic Registration

Introduction

Dependency Injection (DI) simplifies the management of dependencies and promotes modular design. As applications grow, advanced scenarios often demand dynamic modification or extension of services. **Service Decoration** and **Dynamic Service Registration** are powerful patterns that enable flexibility without compromising maintainability.

In this chapter, we will explore:

1. The **Service Decoration** pattern using builder.Services.Decorate.
2. Advanced uses of **Dynamic Service Registration**.
3. Combining these techniques for scalable and adaptable architectures.
4. Real-world use cases and best practices.

1. Understanding Service Decoration

Service Decoration is a design pattern that allows you to wrap existing service implementations with additional behavior dynamically, without modifying the original service or its consumers.

How It Works

When decorating a service:

1. The decorator wraps the original service implementation.
2. The decorator can:
    - Add behavior **before** or **after** calling the original service methods.
    - Conditionally modify the behavior based on runtime conditions.

Use Cases

- **Logging**: Add logs before and after a method call.
- **Caching**: Cache the results of service calls to improve performance.
- **Validation**: Validate input parameters or responses.
- **Authorization**: Check user permissions before invoking the service.

1.1 Implementing Service Decoration

Step 1: Define the Service Interface and Implementation

Service Interface

```csharp
public interface IOrderService
{
    void PlaceOrder(int orderId);
}
```

Original Service

```csharp
public class OrderService : IOrderService
{
    public void PlaceOrder(int orderId)
    {
        Console.WriteLine($"Order {orderId} placed.");
    }
}
```

Step 2: Create the Decorator

A decorator wraps the original service and enhances its behavior.

```csharp
public class LoggingDecorator : IOrderService
{
    private readonly IOrderService _inner;

    public LoggingDecorator(IOrderService inner)
    {
        _inner = inner;
    }

    public void PlaceOrder(int orderId)
    {
        Console.WriteLine("Logging: Starting order placement...");
        _inner.PlaceOrder(orderId);
        Console.WriteLine("Logging: Order placement completed.");
    }
}
```

Step 3: Register Services with Decoration

Use Scrutor's Decorate method to register the decorator.

Setup DI in Program.cs:

```
builder.Services.AddScoped<IOrderService, OrderService>();
builder.Services.Decorate<IOrderService, LoggingDecorator>();
```

When IOrderService is resolved, it returns the LoggingDecorator that wraps OrderService.

1.2 Chaining Multiple Decorators

You can stack multiple decorators for complex behaviors.

Example: Adding Validation and Logging

```csharp
public class ValidationDecorator : IOrderService
{
    private readonly IOrderService _inner;

    public ValidationDecorator(IOrderService inner)
    {
        _inner = inner;
    }

    public void PlaceOrder(int orderId)
    {
        if (orderId <= 0)
            throw new ArgumentException("Order ID must be greater than zero.");

        _inner.PlaceOrder(orderId);
    }
}
```

Registration with Multiple Decorators

```csharp
builder.Services.Decorate<IOrderService, ValidationDecorator>();
builder.Services.Decorate<IOrderService, LoggingDecorator>();
```

Execution Order

1. **ValidationDecorator** validates the input.
2. **LoggingDecorator** logs the process.
3. **OrderService** processes the order.

2. Dynamic Service Registration

Dynamic Service Registration enables services to be registered or replaced at runtime based on configuration, environment, or business logic.

2.1 Dynamic Registration Example

Scenario: Register Services Based on Configuration

```
builder.Services.AddScoped<IOrderService>(sp =>
{
    var configuration = sp.GetRequiredService<IConfiguration>();
    var useAdvancedService = 
configuration.GetValue<bool>("UseAdvancedOrderService");

    return useAdvancedService
        ? new AdvancedOrderService() as IOrderService
        : new OrderService();
});
```

AdvancedOrderService Implementation

```
public class AdvancedOrderService : IOrderService
{
    public void PlaceOrder(int orderId)
    {
        Console.WriteLine($"Advanced processing for order {orderId}.");
    }
}
```

With this setup, OrderService or AdvancedOrderService is dynamically resolved based on a configuration value.

2.2 Runtime Replacement of Services

Scenario: Replacing Services Dynamically

```
public static void ReplaceService<TService, TImplementation>(
    IServiceCollection services,
    ServiceLifetime lifetime)
```

```csharp
    where TService : class
    where TImplementation : class, TService
{
    var descriptor = services.FirstOrDefault(d => d.ServiceType == typeof(TService));
    if (descriptor != null)
        services.Remove(descriptor);

    services.Add(new ServiceDescriptor(typeof(TService), typeof(TImplementation), lifetime));
}
```

Usage

```csharp
ReplaceService<IOrderService, AdvancedOrderService>(builder.Services, ServiceLifetime.Scoped);
```

2.3 Real-Time Registration in Middleware

Services can be conditionally registered or resolved during middleware execution.

Example: Conditional Middleware Registration

```csharp
app.Use(async (context, next) =>
{
    if (context.Request.Headers.ContainsKey("UseAdvanced"))
    {
        using var scope = app.Services.CreateScope();
        var advancedService = scope.ServiceProvider.GetRequiredService<IAdvancedService>();
        advancedService.Execute();
    }
    await next();
});
```

3. Combining Service Decoration and Dynamic Registration

These techniques can be combined for advanced scenarios like multi-tenant systems or feature toggles.

Example: Multi-Tenant Service Decoration

Tenant-Specific Service Implementation

```csharp
public class TenantServiceDecorator : IOrderService
{
    private readonly IOrderService _inner;

    public TenantServiceDecorator(IOrderService inner)
    {
        _inner = inner;
    }

    public void PlaceOrder(int orderId)
    {
        Console.WriteLine("Tenant-specific logic applied.");
        _inner.PlaceOrder(orderId);
    }
}
```

Dynamic Tenant Configuration

```csharp
builder.Services.AddScoped<IOrderService, OrderService>();
builder.Services.Decorate<IOrderService, TenantServiceDecorator>();
```

Real-World Scenario: Feature Toggles with Decorators

FeatureToggleDecorator Implementation

```csharp
public class FeatureToggleDecorator : IOrderService
{
    private readonly IOrderService _inner;
    private readonly IConfiguration _configuration;

    public FeatureToggleDecorator(IOrderService inner, IConfiguration configuration)
    {
        _inner = inner;
        _configuration = configuration;
    }

    public void PlaceOrder(int orderId)
    {
        var isFeatureEnabled = _configuration.GetValue<bool>("FeatureToggles:OrderFeature");
        if (!isFeatureEnabled)
        {
            Console.WriteLine("Order feature is disabled.");
            return;
        }

        _inner.PlaceOrder(orderId);
    }
}
```

Registration

```csharp
builder.Services.Decorate<IOrderService, FeatureToggleDecorator>();
```

4. Best Practices

1. **Decorate Only When Necessary:**
   - Avoid overusing decorators; keep logic focused and modular.
2. **Test Each Layer Independently:**
   - Validate the behavior of each decorator before testing the entire chain.

3. **Use Dynamic Registration Sparingly:**
   - Prefer static registration for predictable behavior; use dynamic registration for specific scenarios.
4. **Combine Patterns Thoughtfully:**
   - Combine service decoration with dynamic registration for multi-tenant or feature-based systems.
5. **Monitor Performance:**
   - Excessive decoration or dynamic resolution can impact performance. Profile critical paths.

Summary

Service Decoration and Dynamic Registration are powerful techniques that enhance flexibility and modularity in .NET applications. By leveraging these patterns, developers can build scalable, maintainable systems that adapt to dynamic requirements. Combining decorators with runtime registration unlocks advanced capabilities, making DI a cornerstone of modern software architecture.

In the next chapter, we will explore **Optimizing Dependency Injection for Performance and Scalability**, focusing on advanced techniques for high-performance DI configurations.

Chapter 18: Design Patterns with Advanced Dependency Injection

Introduction

Design patterns are fundamental to creating scalable, maintainable, and extensible software systems. Advanced Dependency Injection (DI) in .NET simplifies the implementation of complex design patterns, enabling dynamic service resolution, modularity, and flexibility.

This chapter explores:

1. Implementing the **Factory Pattern** for dynamic service creation.
2. The **Strategy Pattern** for flexible behavior injection.
3. The **Decorator Pattern** for extending functionality.
4. The **Proxy Pattern** for controlled service access.
5. Real-world scenarios and best practices for combining design patterns with DI.

1. Factory Pattern with DI

The Factory Pattern simplifies the creation of objects, especially when instantiation logic is complex or dynamic.

Implementation

Step 1: Define a Factory Interface

```
public interface IServiceFactory
{
```

```csharp
    T CreateService<T>();
}
```

Step 2: Implement the Factory

```csharp
public class ServiceFactory : IServiceFactory
{
    private readonly IServiceProvider _serviceProvider;

    public ServiceFactory(IServiceProvider serviceProvider)
    {
        _serviceProvider = serviceProvider;
    }

    public T CreateService<T>()
    {
        return _serviceProvider.GetRequiredService<T>();
    }
}
```

Step 3: Register the Factory

```csharp
builder.Services.AddScoped<IServiceFactory, ServiceFactory>();
```

Step 4: Use the Factory

```csharp
public class OrderProcessor
{
    private readonly IServiceFactory _serviceFactory;

    public OrderProcessor(IServiceFactory serviceFactory)
    {
        _serviceFactory = serviceFactory;
    }

    public void ProcessOrder()
    {
        var service = _serviceFactory.CreateService<IOrderService>();
        service.PlaceOrder();
    }
}
```

2. Strategy Pattern with DI

The Strategy Pattern enables selecting behavior dynamically at runtime by injecting different implementations of a strategy interface.

Implementation

Step 1: Define a Strategy Interface

```
public interface IPaymentStrategy
{
    void ProcessPayment();
}
```

Step 2: Implement Different Strategies

```
public class CreditCardPayment : IPaymentStrategy
{
    public void ProcessPayment() => Console.WriteLine("Processing credit card payment.");
}

public class PayPalPayment : IPaymentStrategy
{
    public void ProcessPayment() => Console.WriteLine("Processing PayPal payment.");
}
```

Step 3: Register Strategies

```
builder.Services.AddScoped<IPaymentStrategy, CreditCardPayment>("CreditCard");
builder.Services.AddScoped<IPaymentStrategy, PayPalPayment>("PayPal");
```

Step 4: Resolve Strategies Dynamically

```csharp
public class PaymentProcessor
{
    private readonly IServiceProvider _serviceProvider;

    public PaymentProcessor(IServiceProvider serviceProvider)
    {
        _serviceProvider = serviceProvider;
    }

    public void Process(string strategy)
    {
        var paymentStrategy =
_serviceProvider.GetRequiredKeyedService<IPaymentStrategy>(strategy);
        paymentStrategy.ProcessPayment();
    }
}
```

Usage

```csharp
var processor = app.Services.GetRequiredService<PaymentProcessor>();
processor.Process("CreditCard");
```

3. Decorator Pattern with DI

The Decorator Pattern dynamically adds behavior to an object by wrapping it in another object.

Implementation

Step 1: Define the Base Service Interface

```csharp
public interface IOrderService
{
```

```csharp
    void PlaceOrder(int orderId);
}
```

Step 2: Implement the Base Service

```csharp
public class OrderService : IOrderService
{
    public void PlaceOrder(int orderId)
    {
        Console.WriteLine($"Order {orderId} placed.");
    }
}
```

Step 3: Implement the Decorator

```csharp
public class LoggingDecorator : IOrderService
{
    private readonly IOrderService _inner;

    public LoggingDecorator(IOrderService inner)
    {
        _inner = inner;
    }

    public void PlaceOrder(int orderId)
    {
        Console.WriteLine($"Logging: Starting order {orderId}.");
        _inner.PlaceOrder(orderId);
        Console.WriteLine($"Logging: Finished order {orderId}.");
    }
}
```

Step 4: Register the Decorator

```csharp
builder.Services.AddScoped<IOrderService, OrderService>();
builder.Services.Decorate<IOrderService, LoggingDecorator>();
```

Usage

```
var service = app.Services.GetRequiredService<IOrderService>();
service.PlaceOrder(123);
```

4. Proxy Pattern with DI

The Proxy Pattern controls access to an object, adding functionality such as caching, authentication, or logging.

Implementation

Step 1: Define the Service Interface and Implementation

```
public interface IDataService
{
    string GetData();
}

public class DataService : IDataService
{
    public string GetData() => "Original data.";
}
```

Step 2: Implement the Proxy

```
public class CachingProxy : IDataService
{
    private readonly IDataService _inner;
    private string? _cachedData;

    public CachingProxy(IDataService inner)
    {
        _inner = inner;
    }

    public string GetData()
    {
```

```
        if (_cachedData == null)
        {
            _cachedData = _inner.GetData();
        }
        return _cachedData;
    }
}
```

Step 3: Register the Proxy

```
builder.Services.AddScoped<IDataService, DataService>();
builder.Services.Decorate<IDataService, CachingProxy>();
```

Usage

```
var service = app.Services.GetRequiredService<IDataService>();
Console.WriteLine(service.GetData()); // Fetches original data.
Console.WriteLine(service.GetData()); // Returns cached data.
```

5. Combining Patterns

Combine patterns for complex scenarios, such as adding a decorator to a factory-produced service or applying a proxy to strategies.

Example: Caching Decorated Strategies

1. Apply a caching proxy to each payment strategy.
2. Use the factory to resolve decorated strategies dynamically.

Registration

```
builder.Services.AddScoped<IPaymentStrategy, CreditCardPayment>("CreditCard");
```

```
builder.Services.AddScoped<IPaymentStrategy, PayPalPayment>("PayPal");
builder.Services.Decorate<IPaymentStrategy, CachingProxy>();
```

6. Real-World Scenarios

1. **Mediator with Strategy:**
   - Use the Mediator Pattern to dynamically resolve and execute strategies.
2. **Proxy for Microservices:**
   - Use a proxy to handle authentication or retry logic for HTTP clients.
3. **Decorator for Validation:**
   - Wrap services with decorators to validate input before execution.

Best Practices

1. **Combine Patterns Thoughtfully:**
   - Use combinations like Factory + Decorator for complex workflows.
2. **Avoid Over-Decoration:**
   - Keep the decoration chain minimal to avoid performance overhead.
3. **Leverage DI for Dynamic Behavior:**
   - Use IServiceProvider or Keyed Services for runtime resolution.
4. **Test Patterns in Isolation:**
   - Mock dependencies to test each pattern independently.

Summary

Advanced Dependency Injection in .NET simplifies the implementation of powerful design patterns like Factory, Strategy, Decorator, and Proxy. These patterns enable dynamic behavior, scalability, and maintainability in modern applications. By leveraging DI, developers can create robust systems that adapt to changing requirements with minimal effort.

In the next chapter, we will explore **Optimizing Dependency Injection for Large-Scale Applications**, focusing on performance tuning, lifecycle management, and advanced configuration techniques.

Chapter 19: Optimizing Dependency Injection for Large-Scale Applications

Introduction

As applications grow in complexity, optimizing Dependency Injection (DI) becomes essential for maintaining performance, scalability, and maintainability. Large-scale systems often involve numerous services, complex lifecycles, and dynamic configurations, all of which can challenge DI containers.

This chapter explores:

1. Performance optimization techniques for DI.
2. Managing lifecycles effectively in large applications.
3. Advanced configuration and dynamic resolution.
4. Handling common pitfalls in large-scale DI setups.
5. Best practices for scaling DI in enterprise applications.

1. Performance Optimization Techniques

1.1 Minimize Service Resolution Overhead

Service resolution can become a bottleneck in large applications. Optimize by reducing the frequency and complexity of service resolutions.

Tip: Avoid Excessive Transient Services

- Transient services are instantiated every time they are requested.

- Use Scoped or Singleton where appropriate to reduce instantiation costs.
- `builder.Services.AddScoped<IOrderService, OrderService>();`

Tip: Precompute Dependencies

- Cache frequently used services instead of resolving them repeatedly.

```
public class CachedService
{
    private readonly IHeavyService _cachedService;

    public CachedService(IServiceProvider serviceProvider)
    {
        _cachedService = serviceProvider.GetRequiredService<IHeavyService>();
    }

    public void UseService()
    {
        _cachedService.DoWork();
    }
}
```

1.2 Use Lazy Initialization

Lazy initialization defers service instantiation until it is actually needed, reducing startup time.

Example: Using Lazy<T>

```
public class ReportService
{
    private readonly Lazy<IDataService> _dataService;

    public ReportService(Lazy<IDataService> dataService)
    {
        _dataService = dataService;
```

```
    }

    public void GenerateReport()
    {
        var data = _dataService.Value.GetData();
        Console.WriteLine(data);
    }
}
```

Registration

```
builder.Services.AddScoped<IDataService, DataService>();
builder.Services.AddScoped(sp => new Lazy<IDataService>(() =>
sp.GetRequiredService<IDataService>()));
```

1.3 Profile and Analyze DI Performance

Use profiling tools like **Visual Studio Profiler, PerfView,** or **Application Insights** to identify bottlenecks in DI.

2. Managing Lifecycles Effectively

2.1 Choose the Right Lifecycle

- **Singleton**: Single instance for the application lifetime.
- **Scoped**: One instance per request (ideal for web apps).
- **Transient**: A new instance every time (lightweight, stateless services).

Lifecycle Example

```
builder.Services.AddSingleton<ISingletonService, SingletonService>();
builder.Services.AddScoped<IScopedService, ScopedService>();
builder.Services.AddTransient<ITransientService, TransientService>();
```

2.2 Scoped Services in Background Tasks

In background services, scoped services must be resolved within a new scope.

Example

```
public class BackgroundTask : BackgroundService
{
    private readonly IServiceProvider _serviceProvider;

    public BackgroundTask(IServiceProvider serviceProvider)
    {
        _serviceProvider = serviceProvider;
    }

    protected override async Task ExecuteAsync(CancellationToken stoppingToken)
    {
        using var scope = _serviceProvider.CreateScope();
        var service = scope.ServiceProvider.GetRequiredService<IMyScopedService>();
        await service.PerformTask();
    }
}
```

2.3 Avoid Circular Dependencies

Circular dependencies occur when two or more services depend on each other.

Detecting Circular Dependencies

System.InvalidOperationException: A circular dependency was detected.

Solution

- Break the cycle using factories or intermediary services.

```csharp
public class ServiceResolver : IServiceResolver
{
    private readonly IServiceProvider _serviceProvider;

    public ServiceResolver(IServiceProvider serviceProvider)
    {
        _serviceProvider = serviceProvider;
    }

    public IService GetService()
    {
        return _serviceProvider.GetRequiredService<IService>();
    }
}
```

3. Advanced Configuration and Dynamic Resolution

3.1 Register Services Dynamically

Dynamically register services based on runtime conditions.

Example

```csharp
builder.Services.AddScoped<IOrderService>(sp =>
{
    var config = sp.GetRequiredService<IConfiguration>();
    return config.GetValue<bool>("UseAdvancedService")
        ? new AdvancedOrderService()
        : new OrderService();
});
```

3.2 Use Keyed Services for Context-Specific Implementations

Keyed services enable dynamic resolution of services based on keys.

Example

```
builder.Services.AddKeyedScoped<IShippingService, AirShippingService>("Air");
builder.Services.AddKeyedScoped<IShippingService, SeaShippingService>("Sea");

var shippingService =
serviceProvider.GetRequiredKeyedService<IShippingService>("Air");
shippingService.ShipPackage();
```

4. Handling Common Pitfalls in DI

4.1 Overusing DI

Avoid over-injecting services into a single class. This indicates poor design.

Solution: Apply the Facade Pattern

```
public class OrderProcessingFacade
{
    private readonly IOrderService _orderService;
    private readonly IShippingService _shippingService;

    public OrderProcessingFacade(IOrderService orderService, IShippingService shippingService)
    {
        _orderService = orderService;
        _shippingService = shippingService;
    }

    public void ProcessOrder(int orderId)
    {
        _orderService.PlaceOrder(orderId);
```

```
        _shippingService.ShipPackage(orderId);
    }
}
```

4.2 Memory Leaks

Memory leaks occur when services are not disposed properly.

Solution: Use IAsyncDisposable

```
public class DisposableService : IAsyncDisposable
{
    public async ValueTask DisposeAsync()
    {
        // Release resources here
    }
}
```

5. Best Practices for Large-Scale DI

1. **Centralize Registration:**
     - Use extension methods to organize service registrations.

```
public static class ServiceCollectionExtensions
{
    public static IServiceCollection AddMyServices(this IServiceCollection services)
    {
        services.AddScoped<IOrderService, OrderService>();
        services.AddScoped<IShippingService, ShippingService>();
        return services;
    }
}
```

2. **Use Dependency Injection Sparingly:**
   - Avoid injecting services unless absolutely necessary.
3. **Monitor Performance:**
   - Regularly profile DI performance in production environments.
4. **Isolate Service Lifetimes:**
   - Ensure correct lifetimes for each service to prevent resource contention.
5. **Test Service Configurations:**
   - Mock services in unit tests to validate DI configurations.

Summary

Optimizing Dependency Injection in large-scale applications requires careful management of lifecycles, dynamic resolution strategies, and performance profiling. By following best practices and leveraging advanced techniques like service factories, keyed services, and scoped management, developers can build scalable and maintainable systems.

In the next chapter, we will explore **Dependency Injection in Cloud-Native Microservices**, focusing on DI practices for Kubernetes, serverless, and distributed systems.

Chapter 20: Dependency Injection in Cloud-Native Microservices

Introduction

Cloud-native microservices are designed to be loosely coupled, independently deployable, and scalable. Dependency Injection (DI) is a cornerstone of microservice design, enabling modularity, testability, and runtime flexibility.

This chapter explores:

1. Using DI in containerized microservices.
2. Integrating DI with cloud-native tools like Kubernetes.
3. Leveraging DI in serverless architectures.
4. Real-world scenarios for DI in distributed systems.
5. Best practices for managing DI in cloud-native environments.

1. Dependency Injection in Containerized Microservices

In containerized environments, DI is critical for managing dependencies like logging, database connections, and configuration services.

1.1 Setting Up DI in a Containerized Microservice

Example: .NET Microservice with DI

Step 1: Define the Service Interface

```
public interface IProductService
```

```csharp
{
    IEnumerable<Product> GetProducts();
}
```

Step 2: Implement the Service

```csharp
public class ProductService : IProductService
{
    public IEnumerable<Product> GetProducts()
    {
        return new List<Product>
        {
            new Product { Id = 1, Name = "Product A" },
            new Product { Id = 2, Name = "Product B" }
        };
    }
}
```

Step 3: Register the Service

```csharp
builder.Services.AddScoped<IProductService, ProductService>();
```

Step 4: Use the Service in a Controller

```csharp
[ApiController]
[Route("api/[controller]")]
public class ProductsController : ControllerBase
{
    private readonly IProductService _productService;

    public ProductsController(IProductService productService)
    {
        _productService = productService;
    }

    [HttpGet]
    public IEnumerable<Product> Get()
    {
        return _productService.GetProducts();
    }
}
```

Dockerfile

```
FROM mcr.microsoft.com/dotnet/aspnet:7.0 AS base
WORKDIR /app
COPY . .
ENTRYPOINT ["dotnet", "MyMicroservice.dll"]
```

1.2 Multi-Tenant Microservices with DI

Handle multi-tenancy by dynamically resolving services based on tenant identifiers.

Example: Multi-Tenant Service

```csharp
public class TenantService : ITenantService
{
    public string GetTenantData(string tenantId)
    {
        return $"Data for tenant {tenantId}";
    }
}

builder.Services.AddScoped<ITenantService, TenantService>();
```

Resolve Tenant Context

```csharp
public class TenantMiddleware
{
    private readonly RequestDelegate _next;

    public TenantMiddleware(RequestDelegate next)
    {
        _next = next;
```

```
    }

    public async Task InvokeAsync(HttpContext context, ITenantService 
tenantService)
    {
        var tenantId = context.Request.Headers["TenantId"];
        var tenantData = tenantService.GetTenantData(tenantId);
        context.Items["TenantData"] = tenantData;

        await _next(context);
    }
}
```

2. Integrating DI with Kubernetes

Kubernetes manages containerized applications, providing features like service discovery, configuration, and scaling. DI integrates seamlessly with these capabilities.

2.1 Using Kubernetes ConfigMaps and Secrets with DI

Example: Inject Configuration from ConfigMap

Create a ConfigMap:

```
apiVersion: v1
kind: ConfigMap
metadata:
  name: app-config
data:
  ConnectionString: "Server=db;Database=app;User=sa;Password=your_password;"
```

Load ConfigMap into the Application:

```
var builder = WebApplication.CreateBuilder(args);
```

```
builder.Configuration.AddEnvironmentVariables();
```

Inject Configuration into a Service:

```
public class DatabaseService
{
    private readonly string _connectionString;

    public DatabaseService(IConfiguration configuration)
    {
        _connectionString = configuration["ConnectionString"];
    }
}
```

2.2 Health Checks and DI

Use health checks to monitor microservice dependencies dynamically.

Example: Adding a Health Check

```
builder.Services.AddHealthChecks()
    .AddCheck("Database", () =>
    {
        // Simulated database health check
        return HealthCheckResult.Healthy();
    });
```

3. DI in Serverless Architectures

Serverless platforms like AWS Lambda and Azure Functions use DI to manage services efficiently.

3.1 Dependency Injection in Azure Functions

Step 1: Configure DI in Startup.cs

```
[assembly: FunctionsStartup(typeof(MyFunctionApp.Startup))]

public class Startup : FunctionsStartup
{
    public override void Configure(IFunctionsHostBuilder builder)
    {
        builder.Services.AddSingleton<IProductService, ProductService>();
    }
}
```

Step 2: Inject Dependencies into a Function

```
public class ProductFunction
{
    private readonly IProductService _productService;

    public ProductFunction(IProductService productService)
    {
        _productService = productService;
    }

    [FunctionName("GetProducts")]
    public IActionResult Run(
        [HttpTrigger(AuthorizationLevel.Function, "get")] HttpRequest req)
    {
        return new OkObjectResult(_productService.GetProducts());
    }
}
```

3.2 Dependency Injection in AWS Lambda

Step 1: Configure DI

```csharp
public static IServiceProvider BuildServiceProvider()
{
    var services = new ServiceCollection();
    services.AddSingleton<IProductService, ProductService>();
    return services.BuildServiceProvider();
}
```

Step 2: Use DI in a Lambda Handler

```csharp
public class LambdaHandler
{
    private readonly IServiceProvider _serviceProvider;

    public LambdaHandler()
    {
        _serviceProvider = BuildServiceProvider();
    }

    public string HandleRequest()
    {
        var productService = _serviceProvider.GetRequiredService<IProductService>();
        return string.Join(", ", productService.GetProducts());
    }
}
```

4. Real-World Scenarios

4.1 Distributed Tracing

Inject tracing tools (e.g., OpenTelemetry) to monitor microservices.

```csharp
builder.Services.AddOpenTelemetryTracing(tracing =>
{
    tracing.AddAspNetCoreInstrumentation()
```

```
            .AddHttpClientInstrumentation()
            .AddJaegerExporter();
});
```

4.2 API Gateway Integration

Inject API Gateway services for authentication, rate limiting, or routing.

```
public class ApiGatewayMiddleware
{
    private readonly RequestDelegate _next;

    public ApiGatewayMiddleware(RequestDelegate next)
    {
        _next = next;
    }

    public async Task InvokeAsync(HttpContext context)
    {
        // Example: Validate API key
        var apiKey = context.Request.Headers["ApiKey"];
        if (string.IsNullOrEmpty(apiKey))
        {
            context.Response.StatusCode = 401;
            return;
        }

        await _next(context);
    }
}
```

5. Best Practices

1. **Use Scopes for Microservices:**
     - Avoid long-lived dependencies; use scoped lifetimes.
2. **Leverage Kubernetes Features:**

- Use ConfigMaps and Secrets for environment-specific configurations.
3. **Minimize Startup Overhead:**
    - Use lazy initialization for expensive services.
4. **Adopt Observability:**
    - Integrate logging, metrics, and tracing into DI.
5. **Secure Secrets:**
    - Never hard-code secrets; use cloud-native secret management tools.

Summary

Dependency Injection is a vital component of cloud-native microservices, enabling modularity, scalability, and testability. By integrating DI with tools like Kubernetes, ConfigMaps, Azure Functions, and AWS Lambda, developers can build resilient, distributed systems. Following best practices ensures seamless deployment and operation in dynamic cloud environments.

In the next chapter, we will explore **Testing and Monitoring DI in Cloud-Native Systems**, focusing on best practices for validating and optimizing DI-based architectures.

Chapter 21: Testing and Monitoring Dependency Injection in Cloud-Native Systems

Introduction

In cloud-native systems, testing and monitoring are critical to ensure the reliability, performance, and scalability of Dependency Injection (DI) implementations. Proper testing validates service configurations and resolves runtime issues, while monitoring provides insights into the system's health, dependency usage, and performance bottlenecks.

This chapter covers:

1. Unit testing for DI-based services.
2. Integration testing in distributed systems.
3. Observability techniques with logging, tracing, and metrics.
4. Tools for monitoring DI in production environments.
5. Best practices for testing and monitoring DI.

1. Unit Testing for DI-Based Services

Unit testing ensures individual services behave as expected, independently of other components.

1.1 Mocking Dependencies

Use mocking frameworks like **Moq** to replace real dependencies with mock objects.

Example: Unit Testing a Service

```csharp
public interface IOrderRepository
{
    void SaveOrder(Order order);
}

public class OrderService
{
    private readonly IOrderRepository _repository;

    public OrderService(IOrderRepository repository)
    {
        _repository = repository;
    }

    public void PlaceOrder(Order order)
    {
        _repository.SaveOrder(order);
    }
}
```

Test

```csharp
[Fact]
public void PlaceOrder_ShouldCallSaveOrder()
{
    // Arrange
    var mockRepo = new Mock<IOrderRepository>();
    var service = new OrderService(mockRepo.Object);
    var order = new Order();

    // Act
    service.PlaceOrder(order);

    // Assert
    mockRepo.Verify(repo => repo.SaveOrder(order), Times.Once);
}
```

1.2 Validating Service Configurations

Ensure DI configurations are correct during testing.

Example: Validate Service Registration

```csharp
[Fact]
public void ServiceConfiguration_ShouldResolveOrderService()
{
    var services = new ServiceCollection();
    services.AddScoped<IOrderRepository, OrderRepository>();
    services.AddScoped<OrderService>();

    var provider = services.BuildServiceProvider();
    var service = provider.GetService<OrderService>();

    Assert.NotNull(service);
}
```

2. Integration Testing in Distributed Systems

Integration testing validates interactions between multiple services and external dependencies like databases, APIs, or message queues.

2.1 Using In-Memory Databases

Test database-dependent services without requiring a real database.

Example: Using In-Memory Database

```csharp
Fact]
public async Task AddOrder_ShouldSaveToDatabase()
{
    var options = new DbContextOptionsBuilder<AppDbContext>()
        .UseInMemoryDatabase("TestDb")
        .Options;
```

```
    using var context = new AppDbContext(options);
    var service = new OrderService(context);

    var order = new Order();
    await service.AddOrder(order);

    Assert.Single(context.Orders);
}
```

2.2 Testing HTTP Interactions

Mock external HTTP APIs using libraries like **WireMock.Net** or **Moq**.

Example: Mocking an HTTP Client

```
[[Fact]
public async Task GetProducts_ShouldReturnProducts()
{
    var mockHandler = new Mock<HttpMessageHandler>();
    mockHandler
        .Setup(handler => handler.SendAsync(It.IsAny<HttpRequestMessage>(), It.IsAny<CancellationToken>()))
        .ReturnsAsync(new HttpResponseMessage
        {
            StatusCode = HttpStatusCode.OK,
            Content = new StringContent("[{\"Id\":1,\"Name\":\"Product A\"}]")
        });

    var client = new HttpClient(mockHandler.Object);
    var service = new ProductService(client);

    var products = await service.GetProducts();

    Assert.Single(products);
    Assert.Equal("Product A", products[0].Name);
}
```

3. Observability with DI

Monitoring DI-based systems ensures that services are operating as expected and aids in identifying issues.

3.1 Logging Dependency Usage

Log service resolutions to understand how dependencies are used.

Example: Add Logging for DI

```
builder.Services.AddTransient<IOrderService, OrderService>()
    .PostConfigure<IOrderService>(service => Console.WriteLine($"Resolved {service.GetType().Name}"));
```

3.2 Distributed Tracing

Use **OpenTelemetry** for tracing service interactions in microservices.

Example: Adding Tracing

```
builder.Services.AddOpenTelemetryTracing(builder =>
{
    builder.AddAspNetCoreInstrumentation()
        .AddHttpClientInstrumentation()
        .AddJaegerExporter();
```

});

Trace Visualizations in Jaeger

- Monitor request flow across services.
- Identify bottlenecks in DI-based service calls.

3.3 Monitoring Performance

Use **Application Insights** to track DI performance and service health.

Key Metrics to Monitor

- Service resolution times.
- Memory usage of Singleton services.
- Request latency for scoped services.

Setup Application Insights

```
builder.Services.AddApplicationInsightsTelemetry();
```

4. Tools for Monitoring DI

Visual Studio Profiler

- Identify DI-related bottlenecks during development.

PerfView

- Analyze CPU and memory usage for DI-heavy services.

OpenTelemetry

- Monitor distributed systems with comprehensive tracing and metrics.

Kubernetes Health Probes

- Use liveness and readiness probes to monitor microservices.

yaml

```
livenessProbe:
  httpGet:
    path: /health/live
    port: 80
readinessProbe:
  httpGet:
    path: /health/ready
    port: 80
```

5. Best Practices for Testing and Monitoring DI

1. **Automate Tests**
   - Automate both unit and integration tests to ensure consistent coverage.
2. **Test Service Lifetimes**
   - Validate that services have correct lifetimes (Singleton, Scoped, Transient).
3. **Log Dependency Resolutions**
   - Log DI resolutions during development to catch misconfigurations.
4. **Implement Health Checks**

        ○ Use health checks to monitor service dependencies in real time.
   5. **Use Metrics and Tracing**
        ○ Integrate metrics and tracing tools for detailed performance insights.
   6. **Simulate Failures**
        ○ Test failure scenarios (e.g., database unavailability) to validate system resilience.

Summary

Testing and monitoring DI in cloud-native systems are essential for maintaining reliability and performance. Unit and integration tests ensure services behave as expected, while observability tools like logging, tracing, and metrics provide critical insights into dependency usage and performance. Following best practices helps build robust, scalable, and maintainable DI-based systems.

In the next chapter, we will explore **Future Trends in Dependency Injection**, focusing on emerging patterns and features in DI frameworks.

Mastering Dependency Injection in .NET 8: Advanced Concepts and Patterns

Chapter 21: Future Trends in Dependency Injection

Introduction

Dependency Injection (DI) has evolved significantly, becoming a cornerstone of modern software development. As application architectures grow more complex, DI frameworks must adapt to address new challenges, such as scalability, modularity, and integration with emerging technologies like serverless and machine learning.

This chapter explores:

1. The evolution of DI frameworks.
2. Emerging patterns in DI.
3. Trends in DI for serverless and cloud-native architectures.
4. The role of DI in machine learning and AI.
5. Future possibilities for DI frameworks.

1. Evolution of DI Frameworks

1.1 Key Milestones in DI

- **Early DI Implementations:**
    - Basic service containers allowed static registrations of services.
- **Integration with Frameworks:**
    - DI became integral to frameworks like ASP.NET Core, Angular, and Spring.
- **Dynamic Resolution:**

- o Features like keyed services and factories enabled runtime flexibility.
- **Observability and Performance:**
  - o Modern DI frameworks now support advanced profiling and metrics.

1.2 Current State of DI in .NET

- **Built-In DI Container:**
  - o ASP.NET Core introduced a lightweight, extensible DI container.
- **Third-Party Enhancements:**
  - o Libraries like Scrutor, Autofac, and Simple Injector offer advanced features like scanning, decoration, and interceptors.
- **Integration with Modern Architectures:**
  - o DI supports serverless, microservices, and event-driven systems seamlessly.

2. Emerging Patterns in DI

2.1 Contextual Dependency Injection

Contextual DI resolves services based on runtime conditions or request metadata.

Example: Contextual Services

```
builder.Services.AddScoped<IShippingService, AirShippingService>("Air");
builder.Services.AddScoped<IShippingService, SeaShippingService>("Sea");

// Resolve based on context
var service = serviceProvider.GetRequiredKeyedService<IShippingService>("Air");
service.ShipPackage();
```

2.2 Polymorphic Registration

Polymorphic registration allows multiple implementations of an interface to coexist, each tailored to specific contexts.

Example: Polymorphic Behavior

```
public interface IDiscountService { double GetDiscount(); }

public class SummerDiscountService : IDiscountService { ... }
public class WinterDiscountService : IDiscountService { ... }

builder.Services.AddScoped<IDiscountService, SummerDiscountService>("Summer");
builder.Services.AddScoped<IDiscountService, WinterDiscountService>("Winter");
```

2.3 DI in Event-Driven Architectures

Emerging patterns focus on dynamically resolving handlers for events.

Example: Event Resolution

```
public interface IEventHandler<TEvent>
{
    Task HandleAsync(TEvent @event);
}

public class OrderPlacedHandler : IEventHandler<OrderPlacedEvent> { ... }

builder.Services.AddTransient<IEventHandler<OrderPlacedEvent>,
OrderPlacedHandler>();

var handler =
serviceProvider.GetRequiredService<IEventHandler<OrderPlacedEvent>>();
await handler.HandleAsync(orderPlacedEvent);
```

3. Trends in DI for Serverless and Cloud-Native Architectures

3.1 Lightweight DI Containers

Serverless platforms like AWS Lambda and Azure Functions prioritize low-latency startup, pushing for lighter DI containers with minimal overhead.

Example: Minimal Dependency Injection

```
builder.Services.AddTransient<IPaymentService, PaymentService>();
```

3.2 Integration with Configuration Services

Modern DI frameworks are integrating deeply with cloud configuration tools like Azure App Configuration and AWS Parameter Store.

Example: Config Integration

```
builder.Configuration.AddAzureAppConfiguration();
builder.Services.Configure<Settings>(builder.Configuration.GetSection("Settings"));
```

3.3 DI in Kubernetes

Kubernetes-native DI solutions manage dependencies across pods and services, enabling seamless updates and scaling.

Example: Service Injection via Kubernetes ConfigMaps

```
apiVersion: v1
kind: ConfigMap
metadata:
  name: app-config
data:
  PaymentService: "AdvancedPaymentService"
```

```
builder.Services.AddScoped<IPaymentService, AdvancedPaymentService>();
```

4. DI in Machine Learning and AI

As machine learning and AI frameworks integrate with general-purpose applications, DI must manage specialized services like model providers, feature extractors, and inference engines.

4.1 Injecting ML Models

DI resolves trained models dynamically based on runtime conditions.

Example: Model Service Injection

```
public interface IModelProvider
{
    PredictionModel LoadModel(string modelName);
}

public class ModelProvider : IModelProvider
{
    public PredictionModel LoadModel(string modelName) { ... }
}

builder.Services.AddSingleton<IModelProvider, ModelProvider>();
```

4.2 Managing Model Lifecycles

Models require efficient memory management and lifecycle handling, which DI frameworks are beginning to support.

5. Future Possibilities for DI Frameworks

5.1 AI-Assisted DI Configuration

AI could assist developers in:

- Automatically detecting circular dependencies.
- Recommending lifetimes (Scoped, Transient, Singleton) based on usage patterns.

5.2 Predictive Service Resolution

Future DI frameworks could preemptively resolve dependencies based on application telemetry, improving performance.

5.3 Fully Decentralized DI

Distributed DI frameworks could span multiple microservices or clusters, resolving dependencies seamlessly across boundaries.

5.4 Enhanced Observability

Next-generation DI frameworks will natively integrate with observability stacks, providing detailed metrics and tracing for service lifetimes and resolution times.

Best Practices for Preparing for Future DI Trends

1. **Modularize Configurations:**
    - Use extension methods to organize and encapsulate service registrations.

2. **Adopt Observability Tools:**
   - Integrate tools like OpenTelemetry and Application Insights to track DI performance.
3. **Embrace Contextual DI:**
   - Use contextual DI to handle dynamic requirements efficiently.
4. **Experiment with Emerging Patterns:**
   - Incorporate new patterns like polymorphic registration and DI in event-driven architectures.

Summary

The future of Dependency Injection is dynamic and promising, driven by the needs of cloud-native, serverless, and AI-driven applications. As DI frameworks evolve, developers must adapt to new patterns and trends to build scalable, maintainable, and high-performing systems. Embracing these advancements ensures that applications remain robust and future-ready.

This concludes our exploration of Dependency Injection. Whether you're building modular desktop applications or highly scalable cloud-native microservices, DI provides the tools and patterns to design clean, maintainable, and testable software systems.

Appendices

Appendix A: Glossary of Terms

This glossary provides definitions for key terms used throughout the book.

- **Dependency Injection (DI)**: A design pattern where an object's dependencies are provided externally rather than being instantiated within the object itself.
- **Service Lifetime**: The duration a service instance exists in a DI container (Transient, Scoped, Singleton).
- **Service Provider**: A container that holds service registrations and resolves dependencies at runtime.
- **Factory Pattern**: A design pattern that uses a method to create instances of a class, often for dynamic resolution.
- **Keyed Services**: A DI feature that allows resolving different implementations of a service based on a key or identifier.
- **Decorator Pattern**: A structural design pattern used to dynamically add behavior to an object by wrapping it in another object.
- **OpenTelemetry**: A framework for observability, providing tools for distributed tracing, logging, and metrics collection.

Appendix B: .NET 8 Dependency Injection Features

A summary of enhancements in .NET 8 related to DI:

1. **Performance Improvements**: Optimized service resolution and reduced memory allocation.

2. **Enhanced Keyed Services**: Built-in support for resolving services by keys or contexts.
3. **Integration with OpenTelemetry**: Simplified tracing for DI-heavy systems.
4. **Minimal APIs with DI**: Streamlined DI usage in lightweight applications.

Appendix C: Tools and Libraries for DI

- **Scrutor**: Extends .NET's DI framework with features like service scanning and decoration.
- **Autofac**: A powerful DI container with advanced lifetime management and module-based configurations.
- **Simple Injector**: A lightweight DI library focusing on simplicity and performance.
- **WireMock.Net**: A tool for mocking HTTP services in integration tests.
- **Jaeger**: A distributed tracing platform integrated with OpenTelemetry.

Appendix D: Example Configurations

Basic DI Setup
```
builder.Services.AddTransient<IOrderService, OrderService>();
```

Service Decoration
```
builder.Services.AddScoped<IOrderService, OrderService>();
builder.Services.Decorate<IOrderService, LoggingDecorator>();
```

Keyed Services
```
builder.Services.AddKeyedScoped<IShippingService, AirShippingService>("Air");
builder.Services.AddKeyedScoped<IShippingService, SeaShippingService>("Sea");
```

Appendix E: Troubleshooting DI

1. **Circular Dependencies**
   - **Issue**: System.InvalidOperationException: A circular dependency was detected.
   - **Solution**: Refactor services to remove direct dependencies or use factories for intermediate resolution.
2. **Service Not Registered**
   - **Issue**: InvalidOperationException: No service for type 'IOrderService' has been registered.
   - **Solution**: Ensure the service is registered in builder.Services.
3. **Memory Leaks**
   - **Issue**: Long-lived services holding references to short-lived dependencies.
   - **Solution**: Use IAsyncDisposable and scoped lifetimes appropriately.

Appendix F: Resources for Further Learning

1. **Books**
   - *Dependency Injection in .NET* by Mark Seemann.
   - *Design Patterns: Elements of Reusable Object-Oriented Software* by Erich Gamma et al.
2. **Online Resources**
   - Microsoft Documentation on DI: docs.microsoft.com
3. **Community Forums**
   - Stack Overflow: Active discussions and problem-solving for DI issues.
   - GitHub Repositories: Open-source projects demonstrating DI implementations.

Appendix G: Advanced DI Patterns Cheat Sheet

Pattern	Description	Example Use Case
Factory Pattern	Dynamically creates objects	Creating database connections dynamically.
Strategy Pattern	Chooses behavior at runtime	Payment gateways (PayPal, Credit Card).
Decorator Pattern	Extends service functionality dynamically	Adding logging or validation to a service.
Proxy Pattern	Controls access to a service	Caching or authentication for APIs.

www.ingramcontent.com/pod-product-compliance
Lightning Source LLC
Chambersburg PA
CBHW062319220526
45469CB00008B/2565